Guide to Board Certification
in Clinical Psychology

Fred L. Alberts, Jr., PhD, ABPP—Dr. Alberts has been in independent practice in Tampa, Florida since 1984. His primary practice is in the area of psychodiagnostics. He is Board Certified in Clinical Psychology and Clinical Child and Adolescent Psychology of the American Board of Professional Psychology. He is Immediate Past Chief of Psychological and Neuropsychological Services at the Tampa General Hospital. He is an Assistant Professor of the Department of Pediatrics, University of South Florida. A Fellow of the American Academy of Clinical Psychology, Dr. Alberts is Past President of the American Academy of Clinical Child and Adolescent Psychology and President of the American Academy of Clinical Psychology. He is author of numerous publications in refereed journals and is Editor of the *Bulletin of the American Academy of Clinical Psychology*. He is also Co-Editor with Theodore H. Blau, PhD, of *The Cue Book: A Courtroom Companion* (Thobois), and the *Forensic Psychology Documentation Sourcebook*—Second Edition (Wiley).

Christopher E. Ebbe, PhD, ABPP—Dr. Ebbe earned a PhD in Clinical Psychology from the University of Missouri at Columbia in 1971. He served seven years in the U.S. Air Force as a psychologist, followed by 30 years as Psychology Training Coordinator for the San Bernardino (CA) County Department of Behavioral Health, treating clients and training new psychologists, including 200 doctoral psychology interns and over 100 post-doctoral residents. Dr. Ebbe is Board Certified (ABPP) in Clinical Psychology (1984) and is Past President of the American Academy of Clinical Psychology (2009–2011). He served as ABPP (Clinical) regional examination coordinator for several years. He also served as President of the Inland Psychological Association (CA) several times. He was awarded the California Psychological Association's *Silver Psi* and several commendations from San Bernardino County for outstanding service. He is currently Chair of ABPP's Council of Presidents of Psychology Specialty Academies. He is the author of *How To Feel Good About Yourself: Twelve Key Steps to Positive Self-Esteem* (2003, 2008).

David B. Kazar, PhD, ABPP—A graduate of the University of Mississippi (Oxford), Dr. Kazar is Board Certified in Clinical Psychology. Dr. Kazar is employed by the Veterans Administration in San Antonio, Texas, where he provides tele-health services and service supervision to outlying facilities. His independent clinical practice spans approximately 20 years, providing assessment and psychotherapy services in various venues and populations, including forensic assessment services. Until recently most of [his] treatment services provided at the Veterans Administration were direct services in the Mental Health Clinic. Dr. Kazar is recipient of APA's *Heiser Award for Legislative Activism* and Past President of the Florida Psychological Association. He is Member-at-Large for Communications of APAs Division on Psychologists in Public Service. He currently is a Fellow of the American Academy of Clinical Psychology, Secretary of the Board of Directors, and serves on the Membership Committee. He is a Member of the Florida Association of Board Certified Psychologists where he serves on the Legislative and Policy Committee and as Representative for Board Certified Clinical Psychologists.

Guide to Board Certification in Clinical Psychology

Fred L. Alberts, Jr., PhD, ABPP

Christopher E. Ebbe, PhD, ABPP

David B. Kazar, PhD, ABPP

SPRINGER PUBLISHING COMPANY
NEW YORK

The book reflects the views and opinions of the individual authors and does not necessarily reflect the policies and opinions of the American Board of Professional Psychology, the American Board of Clinical Psychology, or the American Academy of Clinical Psychology.

Springer Publishing Company, LLC
11 West 42nd Street
New York, NY 10036
www.springerpub.com

Acquisitions Editor: Nancy S. Hale
Production Editor: Joseph Stubenrauch
Composition: diacriTech

ISBN: 978-0-8261-9981-2
e-book ISBN: 978-0-8261-9991-1

13 14 15 / 5 4 3 2 1

The author and the publisher of this Work have made every effort to use sources believed to be reliable to provide information that is accurate and compatible with the standards generally accepted at the time of publication. The author and publisher shall not be liable for any special, consequential, or exemplary damages resulting, in whole or in part, from the readers' use of, or reliance on, the information contained in this book. The publisher has no responsibility for the persistence or accuracy of URLs for external or third-party Internet websites referred to in this publication and does not guarantee that any content on such websites is, or will remain, accurate or appropriate.

Library of Congress Cataloging-in-Publication Data

Alberts, Fred Lee, 1949–
Guide to board certification in clinical psychology/Fred L. Alberts, Jr., Ph.D., ABPP, Christopher E. Ebbe, Ph.D., ABPP, David B. Kazar, Ph.D., ABPP.
    pages cm
  Includes bibliographical references.
  ISBN 978-0-8261-9981-2—ISBN 978-0-8261-9991-1 (ebook)
  1. Clinical psychologists—Certification. 2. Clinical psychology—Standards. 3. Clinical competence—Standards.
  I. Ebbe, Christopher E. II. Kazar, David B. III. Title.
  RC467.7.A43 2013
  616.890076—dc23

                              2013008908

Special discounts on bulk quantities of our books are available to corporations, professional associations, pharmaceutical companies, health care organizations, and other qualifying groups. If you are interested in a custom book, including chapters from more than one of our titles, we can provide that service as well.

For details, please contact:
Special Sales Department,
Springer Publishing Company, LLC
11 West 42nd Street, 15th Floor
New York, NY 10036-8002
Phone: 877-687-7476 or 212-431-4370
Fax: 212-941-7842
E-mail: sales@springerpub.com

Printed in the United States of America by Gasch Printing.

Contents

Foreword

*D*isclaimer: these comments do not represent a dispassionate or unbiased commentary on the important reference book now in your hands. Having obtained five ABPP diplomas between 1977 and 2003, I have perhaps already demonstrated an intense masochistic streak, but more likely revealed a habit that began with collecting merit badges as a Boy Scout. The Board Certification process represents a way to document one's specialized skills and accomplishments through the peer review process. The American Board of Professional Psychology (ABPP) and its component specialty boards represent the premier groups accrediting individual competence in our field as recognized by being the only certification board diplomas in the directory of the American Psychological Association.

My own choices in seeking accreditation unfolded along with the evolution of the ABPP itself. I first learned about ABPP as a student by reading reports in the *American Psychologist* regarding Board Certification as an indicator of excellence in the field, and determined to sit for the examination in the area of my PhD (Clinical Psychology) as soon as I became eligible, five years following receipt of my doctorate. At that time the diploma was offered only in clinical, counseling, school, and industrial/organizational psychology. I worked in a pediatric teaching hospital and Board Certification was the coin of the realm for my physician colleagues.

As new ABPP boards sprang up in forensic, clinical health, couple and family, and clinical child and adolescent psychology I realized that elements of my practice (e.g., child custody evaluations and treating children and families with medical illnesses) reached into those areas and sought some means of professional social comparison to assure that my work met high levels of peer review. In each case the experience of preparing for and following through with the process largely matched the descriptions offered in this book.

Having ABPP certification has proved very valuable for me in several circumstances. Qualifying as an expert witness, renewing hospital privileges, and establishing eligibility for inter-state practice have all been much easier because of holding certification. Several health insurers have also contacted me expressing strong preference for having Board Certified providers on their panels.

Yes, filling out the application and assembling a practice sample can prove time consuming. However, the examination process itself seemed more like a collegial discussion focused on the case material that I had selected to discuss. Some boards add nuances, such as written core knowledge tests in forensic or neuropsychology, but the ultimate outcome remains the same. Colleagues typically emerge from the process feeling a sense of professional validation of their competencies. In addition, the increasing emphasis on quality in health care reform will almost certainly advantage psychologists who become Board Certified. The credential will increasingly become expected as a quality differentiator in the community.

As chronicled by Drs. Alberts, Ebbe, and Kazar the sequence of applying and examination procedures guide participants through a stepwise process with many chances to self-correct, if necessary. Once credential review leads to candidacy, the process of developing and gaining of approval of the practice sample will provide feedback on the adequacy of materials or need for refinement before the oral examination. In preparing this book the highly experienced authors, with many years of service as ABPP examiners, have provided a comprehensive and thoughtful guide to assist you in completing the process successfully.

Gerald P. Koocher, PhD, ABPP
Dean, College of Science and Health, DePaul University
Past President, American Psychological Association

Preface

*D*espite the American Board of Professional Psychology's existence since 1947, the seeking of Board Certification by psychologists in all specialty areas is far less than that of the medical profession. The great majority of physicians practicing a specialty attempt and complete the Board Certification process. Unfortunately, less than 5% of psychologists seek Board Certification in a specialty area at this time. However, clinical work has become very specialized and there is a dramatic and growing need for the identification of those who have met the competency criteria in specialty areas. The authors strongly believe that, in addition to the concrete benefits of Board Certification to the psychologist and the benefits to the public of having competent practitioners identified, there are important benefits of Board Certification to the clients and patients of Board Certified psychologists, since becoming Board Certified reinforces for psychologists the importance of maintaining high standards and the importance of investing in professional development and education throughout one's career. Other books have addressed more general issues (non-specialty specific) in preparing for Board Certification or books on preparation for another specialty area. This book specifically addresses the issues and procedures for the Board Certification process in Clinical Psychology through the American Board of Professional Psychology.

The authors have served as workshop leaders on preparing for Board Certification in Clinical Psychology, mentors for applicants in the process of applying, as examiners and, as a group, have over 60 years of combined practice as Board Certified Clinical Psychologists. The impetus for this book evolved from the authors' experiences fielding questions from potential Board Certification applicants and assisting candidates to navigate the process from application to successful award of Board Certification. As Board Certification in Clinical Psychology is not as widespread and integral a part of one's professional preparation for practice, many eligible candidates for application simply do not understand the application process in its entirety. Some misinformation and lore regarding the process exists, and until one obtains the information from a reliable source, much of the lore and misinformation adds to the anxiety of an already anxiety-producing experience. Our book attempts to clarify the process for Board Certification in Clinical Psychology, dispel some of the myths, and give the reader clear "marching orders" for comprehensive understanding of a method of preparation for the application and examination process.

In Chapter 1, "An Introduction to Board Certification in Clinical Psychology," an overview of Board Certification in health care professions is presented. One frequently asked question is, "Why should I seek Board Certification?" We make an effort to provide the commonly agreed upon benefits of Board Certification and attempt to offer a better understanding of the application process as well as provide real-life experiences. We polled Clinical Psychologists recently Board Certified and gained valuable insights regarding their new self-awareness both personally and professionally. They also report how they think differently about themselves after the process and what they have done differently as a result of the insights gained through the examination process.

Chapter 2 addresses the necessary issues of making the commitment to obtain Board Certification and getting started with the process. Key issues regarding some of the myths of the Board Certification process, attitude toward the process, setting realistic timelines, obtaining a mentor, and other tips for success are provided.

Chapters 3, 4, and 5 address Stages II and III (Practice Samples and Oral Examination). Detailed descriptions of application and assessment components are discussed. In addition to a thorough discussion of intervention and assessment components, examples of application statements and work samples are provided with commentary. Information regarding timelines and scheduling, helpful attitudes toward the oral examination process, preparing for the oral exam, and responses to avoid during the exam are offered.

Maintaining a positive tone throughout the book, the book concludes with a chapter entitled, "Life After Examination." Assuming a successful examination, the authors provide information on becoming a member of the American Academy of Clinical Psychology, opportunities to mentor others, becoming an examiner, promoting

Board Certification, and continuing professional development as Board Certified Clinical Psychologists. Relevant and detailed appendices provide information about the role of mentors in the application process, an example of a contextual statement for an intervention work sample, an oral exam excerpt on an intervention practice sample, and an exam excerpt from the ethical and legal foundations.

From time to time, the American Board of Clinical Psychology, which sets the standards for the Board Certification examination in Clinical Psychology, makes changes to its standards for the examination and its procedures. The material in this book is up to date at its time of publication, and we are committed to revisions of the book to keep it up to date, but we recommend that for examination preparation you use the principles and advice in this book and consult the current *Clinical Psychology Examination Manual* on the www.abpp.org website.

Finally, it is hoped that this book will provide information and motivation to the readers to seek Board Certification in Clinical Psychology. While the authors may maintain active involvement with organizations offering Board Certification or membership services, the opinions expressed and examples provided are the opinions and examples of the authors and not of any specific credentialing or membership organization. The reader is cognizant of the fact that reading this book, following the book's suggestions, or knowledge of examples provided will not be sufficient to establish competence in Clinical Psychology and the reader is responsible for his/her own choices, actions, and results.

The authors wish to acknowledge all of our colleagues who volunteer their time to serve as mentors, examiners, and participate on the American Board of Clinical Psychology and the American Academy of Clinical Psychology. Without our volunteer colleagues and a commitment by those who seek Board Certification to continue the volunteer activities of the Board and Academy, the important process of identifying for the public and our colleagues competent Clinical Psychologists would not exist. The authors would also like to thank their assistant, Ms. Meagan E. Cates, for her helpful work and comments on previous drafts of the book.

Fred L. Alberts, Jr., PhD, ABPP
Christopher E. Ebbe, PhD, ABPP
David B. Kazar, PhD, ABPP

ONE

An Introduction to Board Certification in Clinical Psychology

"It is not the exceptional specialist who should be board certified, but the specialist who is not board certified who should be the exception."
    —Russell Bent, Former Executive Officer, ABPP

I(FLA) have presented many workshops on becoming ABPP Board Certified in Clinical Psychology and Clinical Child and Adolescent Psychology and have often been asked the benefit of becoming Board Certified. Of course the many reasons offered by the board certifying organization are all mentioned at the presentations, plus others, but my story about why I ultimately obtained Board Certification is not an unusual one these days. My mentor was Board Certified in Clinical Psychology and in Neuropsychology, and I recall him often telling trainees and interns, "You're not fit for human consumption until you are five years post-doc." At that time, 5 years was the experience time needed to apply for Board Certification. Now, admittedly, that's a bit harsh, but that was his attitude about identifying and credentialing specialists in Clinical Psychology. To him, you were not a specialist in Clinical Psychology and not prepared to offer services as a specialist until you obtained Board Certification. Thus, I grew up in a culture with an expectation that Board Certification is a necessary, not an optional, aspect of one's professional preparation. With changes in health care and pressures for specialization and subspecialties within professional psychology, the training culture will evolve to meet the demands for measuring training, professional competence, and specialization, and it is expected that Board Certification would then become an expectation rather than purely an option.

I (FLA) also recall that when I first prepared my ABPP application I consulted a graduate school friend who had achieved Board Certification. He was in academia as an associate professor, and I asked for his candid opinion regarding the process. I was not prepared for his response, which was, "Fred, it was the most collegial and beneficial educational experience I have ever had." This was at variance with all of the lore that I had been told about Board Certification. I initially assumed that this was because he was in academia and enjoyed testing and being tested, but the fact is that he was correct. It was the most collegial and beneficial educational experience that I have ever experienced. I have Board Certification from two boards (Clinical Psychology and Clinical Child and Adolescent Psychology). Both examination committees were extremely collegial, and I found the professional discussion with learned colleagues an exceptional opportunity. The self-evaluation process alone, as one develops the application and practice samples, is a worthy process that is both professionally and personally beneficial, and remains one of my fondest memories.

BOARD CERTIFICATION

Board Certification is a way to provide peer and public recognition of demonstrated competencies with primary objectives of ensuring high-quality services for patients and protecting consumers. Medical providers have the longest history of Board Certification, with procedures having been initially established in the early 20th Century. The American Board of Medical Specialties (ABMS) is a group of 24 medical specialty boards, representing 145 medical specialties and subspecialties. Board Certification in the United States is a voluntary process and differs from licensure in that it requires a demonstration to examining peers of a practitioner's exceptional expertise in a specialty or subspecialty area of practice. The designation goes beyond that of medical or professional licensure, which only sets the minimum competencies necessary to diagnose and treat consumers. According to the ABMS, *"The Gold Star (Board Certification) signals a board certified physician's commitment and expertise in consistently achieving superior clinical outcomes in a responsive, patient-focused setting. Patients, physicians, health care providers, insurers and quality organizations look for the Gold Star as the best measure of a physician's knowledge, experience and skills to provide quality health care within a given specialty"* (ABMS, 2012).

Imagine having a medical condition and looking over a short list of physicians to consult regarding your condition and then selecting a physician who is NOT Board Certified in the specialty area of practice. Most informed consumers would want to seek a specialist with Board Certification. Fortunately, most physicians are Board Certified. Estimates are that approximately 85% to 89% of physicians who are licensed to practice in the United States are certified by a specialty board of the ABMS. Now, imagine wanting to refer to a Board Certified psychologist or being a consumer in search of a Board Certified psychologist and understanding that less than 5% of licensed psychologists hold Board Certification in a specialty area. As the health care policies and delivery systems evolve, there is a growing interest and benefit for many health care providers to provide certification of competencies that exceed general state licensure.

Many new models of heath care delivery emphasize the importance of practitioner specialization (Institute of Medicine [IOM], 2004) and focus on ways to both measure and enhance the quality of care. Board Certification is one of the strategies to ensure competence and accountability (Cassel & Holmboe, 2006). While medicine has a very long history of Board Certification, there has been an increase of specialty Board Certification for other medical providers such as nursing, pharmacy, dentistry, physical therapy, and chiropractic medicine, as well as allied health providers such as social work (Dattilio & Sadoff, 2002).

Established in 1947, the American Board of Examiners in Professional Psychology (ABEPP) was established as a credentialing organization within professional psychology. In 1968, the same organization was renamed the American Board of Professional Psychology (ABPP) and continues today as the *"gold standard"* for certifying competencies in professional psychology. Clinical Psychology was one of the original three specialty areas (Clinical, Counseling, and Industrial/Organizational) recognized by ABEPP, thus the assessment of competencies in Clinical Psychology has enjoyed a long history (over 60 years) and has become a valued credential by many of our colleagues. Since the 1980s, the ABPP specialty boards have increased from 4 to 15. Presently, the following specialty areas are under the ABPP umbrella of specialty boards: Clinical Psychology, Counseling Psychology (originally Personnel-Educational and later Counseling & Guidance), Organizational and Business Consulting Psychology (originally Personnel-Industrial and later Industrial Psychology), School Psychology, Clinical Neuropsychology, Forensic Psychology, Couple and Family Psychology (originally Family Psychology), Clinical Health Psychology (originally Health Psychology), Cognitive and Behavioral Psychology (originally Behavioral Psychology), Psychoanalysis in Psychology, Rehabilitation Psychology, Group Psychology, Clinical Child and Adolescent Psychology, and Police and Public Safety Psychology. Later in the process, Academies for the various specialties were established as member organizations for those who have become Board Certified and to promote high-quality practice in those specialties. For a more complete summary of the history of the ABPP, refer to the text, *Becoming Board Certified by the American Board of Professional Psychology* (Nezu, Finch, & Simon, 2009).

The American Board of Clinical Psychology (ABCP), which credentials Clinical Psychologists, is a member specialty board of the ABPP. The ABPP overseas the standards and operations of its 15 member boards.

Psychology is not alone in the professions having witnessed a proliferation of boards and associations providing "diplomate" status, "Board Certification," or "Fellow" status, and so on. Some of these organizations offer the certification and special status without regard to measuring competence or even a thorough credential review. Some believe that holding oneself out as a specialist or holding these credentials without a formal assessment of competence is unethical. In fact, one state, Florida, has a statute with regard to use of terms associated with specialization and/or Board Certification (See Exhibit 1.1).

Exhibit 1.1
490.0149 SPECIALTIES

1. As used in this section, the term "certified psychology specialist," "board certified psychology specialist," or "psychology diplomate" means a psychologist with recognized special competency acquired through an organized sequence of formal education, training, experience, and professional standing that is recognized by a certifying body approved by the board pursuant to criteria adopted under subsection (3).
2. A person licensed as a psychologist may not hold himself or herself out as a certified psychology specialist, board certified psychology specialist, or psychology diplomate unless the person has received formal recognition from an approved certifying body.
3. The board shall adopt rules to establish criteria for approval of certifying bodies that provide certification for specialties in psychology as provided in subsection (1). The criteria shall include that a certifying body:
   a. Be national in scope, incorporate standards of the profession, and collaborate closely with organizations related to specialization in psychology.
   b. Have clearly described purposes, bylaws, policies, and procedures.
   c. Have established standards for specialized practice of psychology.
   d. Provide assessments that include the development and implementation of an examination designed to measure the competencies required to provide services that are characteristic of the specialty area.
4. A person licensed as a psychologist under this chapter may indicate the services he or she offers and may indicate that his or her practice is limited to one or more types of services when this accurately reflects his or her scope of practice.

History.—s. 1, ch. 2006–209.

Regulation of Professions and Occupations - Specialties, Florida Statutes § 490.0149 (2006)

This book, of course, provides information on obtaining Board Certification in Clinical Psychology through the ABPP, the oldest and most acknowledged board for psychologists seeking Board Certification. The ABPP is not only one of the boards on the Florida approved list, but is used as a basis for reciprocity and waiver of some state licensure examination procedures in many states and some Canadian provinces and is the only psychology Board Certifying organization recognized by the Federal Government for employment considerations, including pay grade.

WHY SEEK BOARD CERTIFICATION IN CLINICAL PSYCHOLOGY

Included in application materials for Board Certification in Professional Psychology through the ABPP is a list of *Twelve Reasons to Become Board Certified in Psychology*. The list offers as advantages, among others, the following:

- *Board Certification in Psychology indicates specialty expertise that distinguishes you from other psychologists who work with patients with health issues.*
- *Board Certification in psychology distinguishes you on the job market!*
- *Uniformed psychologists with Board Certification who work at the Department of Defense or Public Health Service receive a monthly specialty pay bonus.*
- *Health care providers in other disciplines consider Board Certification as a minimum standard to document training and expertise for patient care.*
- *Board Certification facilitates license mobility in most states.*
- *Many hospitals ask about Board Certification when applying for privileges.*
- *Some hospitals or medical centers require a Board Certification for approval of privileges, and others are moving toward this policy.*
- *Some academic medical settings require Board Certification for promotion and tenure.*
- *Health insurance companies routinely ask about Board Certification when applying to be part of their networks.*
- *Consumers of health/mental health services will increasingly ask about Board Certification, and can identify Board Certified psychologists online.*
- *Access ABPP online resources for networking and referrals.*
- *Join other leaders in Psychology to define excellence in our field!*

Kaslow, Graves, and Smith (2012) recently summarized and identified key benefits of Board Certification in light of health care reform as follows:

- *Consumers desire specialization*
- *Academic health centers and insurance companies expect Board Certification*
- *Changes in health care call for it*
- *Parity is in our favor*
- *Quality improvement and public accountability programs demand it*
- *Patient-centered health care homes have a place for Board Certified Clinical Psychologists*
- *The workforce needs Board Certified psychologists*
- *Access to care for all is more likely with a well-trained specialty workforce*
- *Integrated health care teams respect Board Certification*
- *Pay is linked to quality*

As noted earlier in this chapter, concrete benefits are not the only reasons to become Board Certified. For most candidates, the idea of high standards for practice and the desire to prove one's adherence to those standards are significant motives. Additionally, many universities, hospitals, health service agencies, and government agencies take Board Certification to be a valuable marker of competence, above the level of state licensure. Thus, Board Certification can set one apart from other applicants for jobs, and in a few instances can result in a pay benefit. Currently, the Department of Defense, Public Health Service, and Veterans Administration have pay differentials for those who are Board Certified.

Many members of the public look for Board Certification in practitioners when seeking services, since they naturally make the analogy between Board Certification in medical specialties and Board Certification in psychological specialties when trying to find the best services for themselves and their families.

Board Certification is a useful credential for establishing one's credibility as an expert court witness, and physicians view it as an important credential when hiring for work in medical settings, including the new "medical homes" that are being established.

Some provider panels prefer Board Certified specialists for providing psychological services to their health plan enrollees. Professional visibility to sanctioners and to the service-seeking public is provided to those who are Board Certified through the online practitioner directories of the ABPP itself and those of the various specialty Academies. Currently 36 of the 50 states make it easier for those who are Board Certified to gain licensure through reciprocity.

Board Certified Clinical Psychologists have the opportunity to publish in the ABPP's journal *The Specialist* and in the *Bulletin of the American Academy of Clinical Psychology*. Also, the cadre of one's Board Certified peers forms a useful and accessible pool of knowledgeable and competent psychologists with whom to consult or refer.

All in all, Board Certification has both meaning and value to offer, and being clear on what you want to gain by becoming Board Certified can help to get you through the several steps of the process.

COMPETENCE

The Ethical practice of professional psychology requires that the individual practice within the limits of his or her competence (American Psychological Association [APA], 2002). Consumers and regulatory bodies have increasingly insisted upon measures of competence in health care delivery systems. Measuring competence achieves the primary goal of protecting the public as well as evaluating the progress of trainees and measuring professional psychology training program effectiveness. We have shifted to a culture of competence and its assessment by identifying key foundational and functional competencies in professional psychology (Fouad et al., 2009; Kaslow et al., 2009; Roberts, Borden, Christiansen, & Lopez, 2005; Rodolfa et al., 2005). Becoming ABPP Board Certified is your route to clearly demonstrating your competence.

WHEN TO BECOME BOARD CERTIFIED

The authors encourage you to apply for Board Certification as soon as you become eligible for application since the inertia of "not right now" and "I'll do it next year" can become harder and harder to overcome. Applications are encouraged, however, at any stage of one's career. Two programs are available that are designed to attract young professionals as well as senior professionals to Board Certification in Clinical Psychology.

Early Entry Program

In order to encourage early entry into the application process, ABPP maintains an Early Entry Program. This Program allows qualified students and other pre-licensed applicants to begin the process toward Board Certification early in one's career. The Program offers a reduced fee for participation and can begin the process of mentoring and ultimately progressing to Board Certification. Applicants under the Early Entry Program may "bank" credentials as they are earned, so as to reduce the necessity to gather these multiple credentials several years later when all application criteria are met.

Senior Option

Psychologists in practice for at least 15 years following licensure at the independent level may be eligible for a senior application and examination process that provides more flexible criteria for eligibility and practice sample requirements, such that the applicant may submit, instead of client videos, a portfolio of written work products that reflect his or her competence (articles, grants, outlines, presentations, etc.). The Practice Samples are reviewed for technical adequacy and a three-member examination committee is established and reviews the Practice Sample for substantive adequacy.

Once the applicant has passed Stage I (Application) and Stage II (Practice Samples), the final stage, Oral Examination, is scheduled. During Stage III, a three-member examining committee conducts an oral examination that is collegial in nature, lasting approximately 3 to 4 hours. The candidate is evaluated in the context of the professional statement and practice sample provided in Stage II. There is no written examination in the Clinical specialty. Once the applicant has passed Stage III, the candidate becomes Board Certified in the specialty of Clinical Psychology. Specific application practice sample requirements are described later in Chapters 3 and 4.

What do Recent Board Certified Psychologists have to say about the process?

Reading books about attaining Board Certification or attending workshop presentations on the topic provide details and hopefully encouragement to those considering applying for Board Certification. However, the perceptions of our colleagues who have gone through the process serve to provide insightful information not otherwise available. To this end, we asked recent Board Certified Clinical Psychologists to respond to a number of questions regarding their experience. Nine psychologists were kind enough to provide us with their comments and we have summarized those below. We find the responses to be overwhelmingly positive and typical of the feedback that we receive when serving as examiners.

Having obtained Board Certification and understanding the process, what were some of the misconceptions that you might have had regarding the Board Certification process?

I anticipated a much more formalized and rigid format for not only the written components of the process, but also for the oral examination. I did not anticipate the flexibility in the approach to the oral examination, nor the interest that my committee had with understanding my role as a psychologist not only with my clients but also to my practice, my surrounding community, and state and national organizations.

The most pleasant surprise for me was the collegial nature of the oral exam. I went in there prepared to re-live a dissertation defense-type examination, but found it quite enjoyable.

I did not anticipate feeling "at peace" when I finished the orals, which was a total surprise. Coming to an understanding of the depth and breadth of my own knowledge and experience was wonderful. Realizing that I had created a mythical "psychologist standard" that was impossibly high and extremely laborious was amusing after the fact.

I have heard some of my peers state that they choose not to seek Board Certification because they do not see an extrinsic need for it. Some have stated that it is only necessary if you work at a VA or in academics. I believe that this misconception might cause someone to miss out on a great opportunity. Board Certification is a rewarding process intrinsically. I do not work at a VA, nor do I work in academics. I think the process offers validation for the hard work and preparation I have put into developing my clinical skills. This process is worthwhile for the confidence and distinction it offers, regardless of the setting one works in.

My biggest apprehension about starting the process was my perception that my skills were not "Board Certification" quality. I believed in a myth, which I felt was supported by the exclusivity that only a small percentage of psychologists are boarded, that those who are boarded are experts in their field and could "talk the talk" far better than I could. Looking back on this process, I believe such myths are the main reason more psychologists do not embark on this process. The process certainly tested my ability to scrutinize my skills, review theory, and brush up on current literature. With commitment to completing this credential, earning your diplomate is most definitely a doable process.

The oral examination was more collegial (more of a discussion about my work than an interrogation) than I anticipated.

How were you able to manage your apprehension or anxiety about showing your clinical work to the examiners?

Quite honestly, the primary motivation for me pursuing Board Certification was because my initial reaction to having my clinical work evaluated was hesitance. Although I was inviting and receptive to feedback and supervision during my graduate training, I recall feeling that my hesitance in being evaluated was something that had grown in me as an independent practitioner since that time. Because I felt then, as I do now, that hesitance was never something any psychologist at any time in [his or her] career should ever experience at the suggestion of being evaluated, I pursued Board Certification.

While it was initially rather anxiety provoking to be submitting samples of my work again, like I had to while in graduate school, I reminded myself that I had much more experience at this point in time and had several years to work on my weaknesses. I told myself that if I did not pass the sample, I would have received constructive feedback that I could incorporate in future attempts. Beyond that, I just took some time to think about my prior successes while in clinical settings, reviewed the provided grade sheets, and had confidence that I could pass.

I did the Senior Option, so I did not have to share a videotape of my clinical work. I did share work samples from various seminars, presentations, etc. I wasn't particularly apprehensive about that part of the process. My anxiety was regarding the oral exam and my anticipation of feeling "on the spot," as well as concern that I would be able to accurately and sufficiently convey my knowledge. I spoke with a number of colleagues about my responses to the Personal Statement and also requested feedback from a Division 42 "Board Certification mentor," which was very helpful. The Chair of my Orals Committee was extremely helpful when he set up the exam, reminding me that I would be presenting as the "expert" of my own work. Framing the oral exam in that fashion was very reassuring. Right before the orals (while waiting to be called into the room), I began to experience some unsettling anxiety. I utilized a five-minute meditation application on my phone, did some positive self-affirmations, and reminded myself of all I had learned going through this process, which was really the point. When I left the orals, I felt awesome! I knew I had presented myself to the best of my ability—and that if there was an area I didn't pass, I was committed to addressing that area and continuing to move forward. While I was extremely happy to receive notification of passing, the actual experience of preparation and doing the oral exam was of equal, if not more, value than the actual outcome.

A friend and I went through it together and I definitely over-prepared. I purchased a new book on ethics and talked to people who had already been through the process.

I usually funnel my anxiety into work. Optimal levels of anxiety helped me to prepare for my oral exam and review my work to ensure that it was a good example of my actual practice. I shared with several of my peers that I was going through the process, and it was helpful to receive from them support and encouragement. They helped me to make sure that I was making the best of those optimal levels of anxiety, and not be overwhelmed by it by reminding me to put things into perspective.

There was one particular line in the ABPP-CP exam prep materials that stood out to me: "Candidates are encouraged to submit practice samples that reflect their competence and expertise (typical rather than exemplary situations are expected)." This statement, along with the continued emphasis on the notion this is a collegial progress, helped reduce my anxiety. It tempered my anxious worries [that] the examiners expected perfection, but rather wanted to see a good product that was reflective of my typical work with patients. Having been through the ABPP process, I can also absolutely attest the examiners mean every word they say about the examination being a collegial process.

I worked closely with another psychologist to set specific deadlines so that I would not procrastinate.

I reminded myself of how desensitized to oversight I was as a student and intern. Supervision, including peer supervision, is a cornerstone of professional growth in psychology. I also assured myself that the tone was meant to be collegial.

What advice might you provide to a candidate for Board Certification in Clinical Psychology?

Based on my experience, I would tell a candidate that the written component helps the committee understand what you know, and the oral examination helps them understand who you are. So for the written component, write what you know; for the oral examination, trust your knowledge, clinical judgment, and instincts, and simply show them who you are.

I think it is important to make completion of the Board Certification requirements a priority. I would recommend spending a day or two every few weeks working on the written portions and making sure you give yourself several months to complete the requirements so that you are comfortable and confident in your submitted samples.

I would say "Go for it!" I have encouraged many people to consider Board Certification and am happy to share my experience with the process. I think many people share the myth of Board Certification being extremely difficult, labor intensive, and judgmental. Particularly as someone who has been licensed over 15 years, the idea of presenting my work to three other people initially seemed very intimidating and scary. It raised internalized doubts I had not previously confronted or addressed. This was a fantastic opportunity to banish those concerns.

Understand the relationship between theoretical orientation and treatment, make sure your treatment protocol acknowledges current research, and demonstrate full multicultural competence.

I found it helpful to break the process down into three distinct phases, and to focus only on the present phase. Looking at the entire process can be overwhelming. This initial phase, completing the application is like jumping into a pool on a sunny day. It does not take too long and is done best by blindly plunging in. Apprehension is probably the largest barrier at this point. Once I began with this commitment, it made it easier to continue with the rest of the process. I would not recommend worrying about Practice Samples at this phase. The Practice Sample phase is where the grunt work comes in. For me, procrastination was a greater enemy than apprehension. I found it helpful to share with a few colleagues that I had started the process so they could provide me with accountability. Second, I created some deadlines for myself by breaking the task into smaller parts. I set a deadline for recording each sample, one for the writing associated with each sample, one for the professional summary, and one for reviewing and sending in the entire packet. Sticking to these deadlines was essential, as it is very easy to get caught up in other responsibilities. For the Oral Examination component the greatest barrier was anxiety and feeling overwhelmed. I found it very helpful to sit down with the ABPP oral examination guidelines, so I was familiar with the criteria I was going to be rated on, and review my samples. It was also helpful to sit down with the APA code of ethics. I found this reviewing process was confidence building for me, as it helped me to feel that I was prepared for the types of questions I was going to be asked.

Appreciate the process of the experience, as that is where the value lies. I spent several months engaged in the process, both "internally" and "externally." The internal aspect involved taking a critical look at myself broadly as a professional, then specifically as an administrator, faculty member, and clinician. What do I do in each of these areas and how is what I do a trajectory of what I was trained to do? How do I demonstrate competency in each of these areas? How do I demonstrate being a lifelong learner in each of these areas? What are my professional strengths, weaknesses, and areas for further development? The external aspect involved extensive review of the Board Certification book, the ABPP website, and the application materials; engaging in professional conversations with colleagues about what I do and what I think about professional issues; even engaging in professional "conversations" and mock interviews with myself as I drove in my car! Throughout the process, I spent time working on the Professional Statement questions. There were multiple drafts of initial thoughts, outlines, and essay content. It was also important for me to step away from the process and the materials a few times, in order to return with a fresh eye and some objectivity. Every moment spent was time well spent, and though I was nervous about the oral exam, by the time I scheduled my exam, I was confident that my materials well-reflected the hard work and thought that I had put into the process, and into the profession, as well as my achievement. Although I had no idea how the exam would go, I was very satisfied with my process and my product; I'm sure that knowing that I had taken the time and the energy to give 100% to the process and the product served to enhance my performance in the oral exam.

I would strongly encourage a candidate to talk with a formal or informal mentor (someone who has recently completed this process) openly about your anxieties and seek any reassurances along the way; there can be long delays from when you submit work sample materials, and a mentor can help put your negative worries in check (delays are not correlated with good or bad results!).

Take a thorough and thoughtful approach. Answer all of the questions asked and provide all required elements.

How do you think differently about yourself now that you are Board Certified?

Becoming Board Certified has certainly given me a certain level of confidence as both a psychotherapist as well as a consulting psychologist in how I apply my clinical judgment and make determinations regarding client care, because of the high standard and quality in our work that Board Certification requires.

I now feel much more confident in my ability as a Clinical Psychologist. Going through this process and being tested by Board Certified psychologists has helped me gain a greater sense of competence and in some instances, expertise.

I am very proud of my Board Certification. I see myself as a strong, competent psychologist and I appreciate the validation within psychology from getting the ABPP. This was really a process that I undertook for myself. I did not anticipate any external changes as a result of Board Certification (pay, status, etc.). I work for a state agency, so there has not been any work-related benefit. Although my achievement was announced within the agency, there is very little understanding of psychology Board Certification.

It definitely means something to me—a peer validation of my competence.

The process has given me greater confidence in my abilities and in my knowledge. I take pride in my ABPP distinction, and feel that it helps me to display professionalism and confidence to my peers and clients.

I walk taller among my peers with the confidence in knowing I have credentials to attest for my ability. I always believed I was a "good" therapist, but in our individual practice we can isolate from colleagues and lose that comparative edge. However, having earned my Diplomate, now I <u>know</u> I am a good therapist.

I feel more confident as a provider and supervisor. The credential has resulted in more requests for consultation, supervision, and provision of additional clinical services.

I am proud of my accomplishment and designation that truly sets me apart as having achieved another level of certification. As the only Board Certified psychologist in my division, I feel it highlights my expertise and leadership abilities.

I now feel more confident that I still have skills to offer, and I am taking steps to act on that confidence. I am taking steps to make others aware of my availability.

What have you found to be most valuable or rewarding about Board Certification?

The most rewarding thing about Board Certification for me was reaffirming confidence in my ability as a psychologist and a psychotherapist, reassuring that I have taken advantage of all available opportunities to develop my ability, and the knowledge that no matter how long I work in this profession, I will never forget to view myself as an evolving psychologist.

I have not experienced any external rewards (salary, referral, colleague acknowledgment). I have received invaluable internal rewards—an increase in self-confidence, a greater sense of mastery, pride of accomplishment, and appreciation of a wonderful learning opportunity.

My school was so validating! The president of the college sent me a dozen roses!!!!!!

As noted above, confidence in my professional abilities, and the recognition from my peers at my office and in the community have been the greatest rewards.

Pursuing Board Certification was very important to me and the motivation was my own. However, I was pleasantly surprised and absolutely delighted by the affirmation and accolades I received from colleagues, friends, and the administration at my institution, all who regarded this as a significant accomplishment in my career.

Though one of the initial reasons I applied for Board Certification was for a salary increase (which certainly has been appreciated!), increased confidence, self-esteem, and validation are clearly my top three rewards after being boarded. A sentiment I share with many colleagues is that graduate school can embed a core belief of doubt in your mind, making you second guess yourself and talk with a degree of hesitancy. Having earned my ABPP, such thoughts are history!

A great sense of accomplishment!

It serves as an objective measure of my expertise in my field. I feel it gives me credibility with my peers, professional colleagues, and patients.

Have you done anything differently as a result of your insights gained through the exam process and, if so, what?

As a psychologist in my practice, I have encouraged the development of clinical team meetings to discuss approaches and techniques that we use in our work with clients. As a supervisor, I have stressed the importance to interns and postdoctoral students of the importance of remaining receptive to feedback regarding their work, not only as training psychologists, but also the importance of maintaining the practices of self-examination and seeking supervision or consultation with colleagues throughout the course of their careers.

I have taken more professional risks—submitting proposals to committees, conferences, journals, etc. I have also approached insurance companies and attempted to negotiate higher rates of reimbursement. Although I have not been successful with this, it has also provided the impetus to remove myself from the lowest-paying panels.

Taken more appropriate professional risks.

I have made a greater commitment to reviewing professional books and literature to continue improving my techniques. Admittedly, this tapered after graduation and in my early years of practicing, but the insight gained through my exam process reminded me how valuable (and easy) such reviews can be!

———————————————

I would have started the process sooner. For several months, a colleague and I put off completion of the paperwork, due to feeling intimidated. Once we got started, the process ran smoothly.

———————————————

I am more committed to sharing my expertise with others – colleagues, interns, fellows.

———————————————

I am a bit more self-assured. I have taken [on] younger psychologists to mentor.

———————————————

The authors wish to thank the following Board Certified Psychologists for their responses and insights: Kyle A. Grohmann, PhD, ABPP; Kristina M. Hallett, PhD, ABPP; Terry Johnston, PhD, ABPP; Susan K. McGroarty, PhD, ABPP; Kevin P. Newgren, PsyD, ABPP; Cheryll R. Rothery, PsyD, ABPP; Paul A. Smiley, PsyD, ABPP; Sarah E. Spain, PhD, ABPP; and Sharlene D. Wedin, PsyD, ABPP.

GETTING STARTED

In the next chapter, "Making the Commitment to Obtain Board Certification and Getting Started," you learn the process required to achieve your destination. The chapter provides an overview of the various stages of examination (the application, the Curriculum Vitae and Professional Statement, Practice Samples of your work, and Oral Examination). You will be provided resources so that you may better understand and prepare for the examination ahead. Then, the following three chapters ("Professional Statement and Curriculum Vitae," "Practice Samples, Focusing on Assessment and Intervention," and "Oral Examination") provide details about each stage of the examination process so that you better understand the process and can maximize and optimize your preparation for it, as well as reduce the anxiety associated with the examination process.

REFERENCES

American Board of Medical Specialties. (2012). What Board Certification Means. *American Board of Medical Specialties.* Retrieved from http://www.abms.org/about_board_certification/means.aspx

American Psychological Association. (2002). Ethical principles of psychologists and code of conduct. *American Psychologist, 57,* 1060–1073.

Cassel, C. K., & Holmboe, E. S. (2006). Credentialing and public accountability: A central role for board certification. *JAMA, 295,* 939–940.

Dattilio, F. M., & Sadoff, R. L. (2002) Mental Health Experts: Roles and Qualifications for Court. Mechanicsburg, PA: PBI Press.

Fouad, N. A., Grus, C. L., Hatcher, R. L., Kaslow, N. J., Hutchings, P. S., Madson, M., ... Crossman, R. E. (2009). Competency benchmarks: A model for the understanding and measuring of competence in professional psychology across training levels. *Training and Education in Professional Psychology, 3,* S5–S26.

Institute of Medicine. (2004). *Academic health centers: Leading change in the 21st century.* Washington, DC: National Academy Press.

Kaslow, N. J., Graves, C. C., & Smith, C. O. (2012). Specialization in psychology and health care reform. *Journal of Clinical Psychology in Medical Settings, 19,* 12–21.

Kaslow, N. J., Grus, C. L., Campbell, L. F., Fouad, N. A., Hatcher, R. L., & Rodolfa, E. R. (2009). Competency assessment toolkit for professional psychology. *Training and Education in Professional Psychology,* 3(4 Suppl), 527–545.

Nezu, C. M., Finch, A. J., Jr., & Simon, N. P. (Eds.). (2009). *Becoming board certified by the American Board of Professional Psychology.* New York: Oxford.

Regulation of Professions and Occupations - Specialties, Florida Statutes § 490.0149 (2006)

Roberts, M. C., Borden, K. A., Christiansen, M. D., & Lopez, S. J. (2005). Fostering a culture shift: Assessment of competence in the education and careers of professional psychologists. *Professional Psychology: Research and Practice, 36,* 355–361.

Rodolfa, E. R., Bent, R. J., Eisman, E., Nelson, P. D., Rehm, L., & Ritchie, P. (2005). Fostering a culture shift: Assessment of competence in the education and careers of professional psychologists. *Professional Psychology: Research and Practice, 36,* 347–354.

TWO

Making the Commitment to Obtain Board Certification and Getting Started

MOTIVATION TO BECOME BOARD CERTIFIED

It is valuable to first examine your motives for becoming Board Certified, since this clarification can help considerably in keeping you focused and committed as you progress toward the ultimate goal. Many of those who become Board Certified do so because Board Certification is recognized as the highest level of expertise in psychological specialties. State licensing examinations do little to assess clinical competence, and Board Certification is the closest we have to a standard put forth by the profession itself to recognize exceptional competence. The American Board of Professional Psychology (ABPP) exams are much more clinically meaningful than state licensure exams, and having the earned stamp of approval of one's professional peers can count for much more than simply being licensed to practice. Some psychologists are motivated simply to test themselves against the highest standard available, while others seek the more concrete benefits that Board Certification can bring (see Chapter 1), and keeping these in mind can help steady your motivation to become Board Certified yourself.

AN OVERVIEW OF THE PROCESS

The examination process in Clinical is designed and carried out by the American Board of Clinical Psychology (ABCP), which is one of the 15 member boards of ABPP. The Examination Manual for ABPP exams in Clinical is posted on www.abpp.org. The Manual (American Board of Clinical Psychology, 2011) contains virtually all of the information you will need about the details of application, Practice Samples, test domains, scoring of exams, forms, appeals, and so on.

Stage I—Credentialing

Credentialing is the first step of the process. There are two application forms, one for ABPP itself that is standard for all specialties and one for the ABCP (both available on www.abpp.org; click on "Applicants" at the top for the general application, and on that page click on Clinical Psychology and then on "Application").

Your degree, internship, license, and current practice are examined through the application process. You must be licensed as a psychologist in order to become Board Certified (but note that with the Early Entry Option, graduate students may begin compiling records relevant to application even before graduation). It helps to have an American Psychological Association (APA) accredited degree and internship, but equivalency is routinely evaluated for other graduate schools and internship programs.

For Clinical Psychology applicants, three years of experience are required, one of which may be pre-doctoral. A one-year formal post-doctoral program (an actual training program and not just pre-licensure employment) can count for two post-doctoral years of the required experience. At least two of the three required years must be supervised by a psychologist. The ABPP Central Office reviews the applications.

If you are reasonably confident, based on the criteria in the Exam Manual, that you will be accepted as a candidate while you are waiting for your application to be approved, you can start to plan your Practice Samples.

Stage II—Practice Samples

Your Curriculum Vitae (CV), a Professional Statement, and two video Practice Samples must be submitted, and these will be the basis of the second stage of the exam. A Committee of three examiners will be appointed, who will examine these items and will determine pass or fail for this stage of the exam (without interaction with you). This same Committee will examine you for Stage III, the oral exam. Any ABPP Board Certified Clinical Psychologist can serve as an examiner, but someone with significant experience with the exam will serve as chair. The Committee will not necessarily be comprised of psychologists with the same orientation or practice areas as yours, but they will be competent to evaluate your knowledge and skills. Be sure that you review and update your CV for clarity. The Professional Statement is an approximately 10-page (double-spaced) presentation of your responses to a number of specific questions regarding your practice and your behavior and attitudes toward the profession, ethics, diversity, and so on. The required content is listed in the Exam Manual (and in Chapter 3 of this book).

The recorded Practice Samples are unrehearsed, 1-hour videos of you with a client, and they may portray (1) evaluation (intake, interview, testing, exam, etc.), (2) intervention (therapy, etc.), (3) consultation (in which the candidate serves as a consultant), or (4) clinically relevant supervision activities (in which the candidate is the supervisor). You must submit samples from two of these four areas, and they must be of work with different clients. The video Practice Samples are your opportunity to show the Committee how you practice, so choose work and clients that tell the Committee the most about you and portray your skills to the best advantage.

You will also submit a Contextual Statement (1,000–1,500 words) for each sample, providing specific required content and explaining the context and any unusual occurrences during the videos. (The required content for these is in the Exam Manual.) Your materials are rated by the Committee members on each of the competency domains listed in the Manual.

The Stage II process is likely to take several months, which includes submission of your package (three copies of everything) to the ABPP Central Office, appointment of the Committee, mailing of your materials to the examiners by ABPP Central Office, time for them to properly examine the content and reach a decision, and notifying you of the result. While you are waiting, you may gather information and plan your preparations for the oral exam.

Stage III—Oral Examination

The oral exam Committee will be the same as the Stage II Committee. The 3-hour oral exam may be scheduled at regular ABCP meeting times in the spring and fall of each year, or in conjunction with the APA Convention, the ABPP Institute held each spring or summer, or regional professional meetings. It may also be scheduled specifically for you at some other time in a nearby city that all examiners can readily reach.

During the exam, the Committee will spend some time getting to know you (from your CV and Professional Statement), discuss with you details from your recorded Practice Samples (exploring your understanding of the theory and model of intervention that you use and its scientific basis, how you apply the model in real life, how you decide on a match between approach and client needs, etc.), and explore with you your response to the ethics situation you described in your Professional Statement and to an ethics vignette provided to you during the exam. The typical schedule for the exam is described in Chapter 5 (and in the Exam Manual, of course).

KNOWLEDGE, SKILLS, AND ATTITUDES SUPPORTIVE OF BOARD CERTIFICATION

One of the purposes of Board Certification is the identification of high standards for professional practice and competence. If you have knowledge, skills, and attitudes that are consistent with high standards, this will make it likely that you will pass the exam. The goals of Board Certification are consistent with the ideals and practices identified in the APA code of ethics. The primary goal of standards for competence in professional practice is to maximize benefit to the client without bringing harm.

In order to provide high quality services, the psychologist must have the requisite knowledge of human behavior and psychological methods. This will be evaluated in the exam primarily by how well you can articulate your understanding of human behavior (in terms of accepted theories and constructs, which can include an eclectic but coherent set of theoretical concepts) and how well you can explain to the Committee your application of those theories and constructs to actual clients. This knowledge includes the scientific underpinnings of and support for your assessment and intervention methods.

Since many of our personal feelings and attitudes significantly affect our practices, the competent Clinical Psychologist must make use of his capacity for accurate self-observation and self-reflection. This is especially true for the individual private practitioner, who typically has only a small amount of interaction with other practitioners. This means being aware of your feelings and behavior, how your feelings are affecting your work, and how your work is affecting your clients.

The competent Clinical Psychologist must be adequately prepared in both attitude and knowledge to provide quality services to persons with personal characteristics and cultural backgrounds that are different from her own. For most of us, this is a long-term process of learning and attitude adjustment—gaining specific knowledge of other cultures and learning how to interact at a human level in ways that do not require cultural concordance.

The competent Clinical Psychologist must genuinely want to benefit his clients and must genuinely wish not to cause them harm or pain. Ethical principles elaborate on how to accomplish these ends, but the desires to help and not to harm must be fundamental to the person of the psychologist. An important attitude for ethical practice is believing that you are accountable for the effects of your behavior and services on others.

Since one's career involves lifelong learning (since there is always more that we can learn), a positive attitude toward ongoing learning and personal development is essential to maximize one's effectiveness. Ongoing learning and personal development means developing new skills and reducing the negative impact on clients from one's counterproductive attitudes and countertransferential behaviors. This openness should extend as well to differences between people in general and differences between ourselves and our clients in particular. There is an appropriate humility to knowing that we are still imperfect and do not know everything.

Objectivity and reasonableness are appropriate in a field in which theories can never be proven and in which treatment methods are subject to constant reformulation and improvement. Don't get so committed to your own views that you cannot see the reasons for and the benefits of the views of others. Don't stop trying to make your own views more accurate and comprehensive. Treating people in general with respect and courtesy illustrates our views on human rights and how we are likely to treat clients. The examining committee deserves this same respect and courtesy.

Being the best professional psychologist that one can be involves not only providing services to clients but also nurturing and advocating for the profession. Any profession needs re-evaluation and refinement from within, as it strives to become more effective and ethical in its provision of services. Psychology, as a profession that concerns itself with helping people live good and healthy lives, has a role in objectively educating society about how to create a social environment that nourishes good and healthy people. The profession must also let society know what it needs to carry out its activities (provide services, educate, research) and must ensure that its legitimate and ethical purposes are adequately supported. Board Certified psychologists may contribute to the profession by being active in and supporting professional organizations and their legislative and lobbying efforts, and by contributing to discussions of important issues for the profession, as well as by serving as Board Certification examiners, working to promote Board Certification, and serving as mentors for Board Certification candidates.

MYTHS REGARDING BOARD CERTIFICATION

There are several enduring but false myths regarding ABPP Board Certification. Many students and psychologists have heard these myths and have been deterred, unnecessarily, from entering into the Board Certification process. You may have heard some of these deterrents from your own professors, colleagues, or supervisors, but be open to reconsidering.

1. Some have thought that the standard (passing level) for Board Certification was too high. While it is true that the standard grew higher from 1947 to 1991, and true that the word "excellence" was then used with regard to the desired level of clinical services of Board Certified psychologists, thousands of psychologists passed the exam at that level, suggesting that it was not

necessarily "too high." In 1992 the standard was redefined to aim at "high quality" services, which was conceptualized as being higher than the level required for licensure but within the reach of most practitioners. The pass rate in Clinical Psychology has been between 85% and 95% for the past several years. I (CEE) have personally mentored quite a few candidates for the exam, and none of them has complained that the level required was unreasonable or too high.

2. Another myth has been that ABPP was a kind of "old boy's network," such that only those who were "in" in terms of their graduate schools and advisors would pass the exam. I suspect that long ago, when psychology was small enough that "everybody knew everybody," where one went to school and one's references counted for more. In this day and age, that is totally impractical, and I can say with certainty that this myth does not apply in any way in the clinical specialty.

3. Some practitioners who choose not to attempt Board Certification have criticized ABPP as trying to create an elite cadre of psychologists who are seen as better than other psychologists and should be given preference and priority for clients and status. There are certainly many psychologists who would prefer that their doctoral degrees and licensure, by themselves, be considered satisfactory evidence of competence, but it is quite clear that the demise of the oral licensure exams marked the end of any argument that licensure certified competence.

Many graduate schools have been guilty of passing on responsibility for quality control to internships and licensing boards and of thereby graduating students with marginal or even inadequate clinical skills. For-profit graduate schools in particular face the dilemma of losing tuition payments if they "flunk out" students. Most internship supervisors want to be "good guys" and are loathe to fail an intern. The EPPP exam tests psychological knowledge but only marginally addresses the kinds of knowledge, insight, and relationship skills that are necessary for competent practice. ABPP and APA were allies in the original establishment of Board Certification (before licensure was established), and while it was thought appropriate at that time for the standards to be set and exams given by an organization separate from APA, ABPP seeks the same quality of preparation and quality of services as APA (as elaborated in APA's code of conduct and in APA's program accreditation standards) and remains the profession's single attempt to certify competence. Licensure's appropriate job is to protect the public from victimization and from shoddy services, but it should be the profession's job to set standards for competence.

4. A particularly deterring myth is that taking the oral exam is a humiliating inquisition, where supposed experts expose your smallest failures in knowledge and technique. No one would wish that upon themselves, but in fact, it is not at all true. It is possible, of course, to get one examiner who does not adhere well to the instructions to establish rapport, treat the candidate as a colleague, and evaluate the candidate in terms of her own theoretical orientation, but this is rare. Candidates are to be treated with respect and courtesy. Most psychologists are eager in their practices and supervision to have the people they are working with succeed, and it is the same with examiners. The feedback we receive on the clinical exam is almost universally that the exam was a collegial learning experience and that the examiners raised questions well worth further consideration after the exam.

ATTITUDE TOWARD THE PROCESS

It is very helpful to approach Stage II and Stage III exam preparation with the intent to, as much as possible, make it an exploration and a learning experience. In deciding on your particular Practice Samples, in viewing them afterward and writing their Contextual Statements, and in rehearsing some of your orals answers, you can find out a fair amount about your strengths, weaknesses, and predilections as a clinician, which is knowledge that you can use to choose areas for further self-observation, practice, and learning.

Learning about yourself in the ABPP process, though, requires self-reflection—the willingness and ability to look at oneself objectively and relate what one sees to clear standards (one's own as well as the profession's). Self-reflection is now recognized as an important aspect of ongoing practice (viz. the recent APA benchmarks of competence), particularly since in our profession one can practice for years (in private practice or in agency practice) with no one observing one's work at all. Self-evaluation for purposes of improvement works even better if you expose your work to others, too, through a peer consultation group or the use of videos with a trusted adviser or colleague (and not just for the ABPP exam).

In assessing one's professional strengths and weaknesses, it may be useful to consider the competency scoring areas for the examination itself. Immediately below are the current competency areas that are the basis for the exam. The ABCP has made a commitment to change these areas in the future to conform to the competency benchmark areas defined by the Competency Benchmarks Work Group sponsored in 2006 by APA's Board of Educational Affairs, as set forth in Fouad et al. (2009).

The first seven of these are termed *"Foundational Competencies"* and the remaining eight are termed *"Functional Competencies."* In the article, behavioral examples are provided for readiness for practicum, readiness for internship, and readiness for entry to practice, but ABCP will probably develop behavioral pass-fail examples for readiness for entry into the specialty of Clinical Psychology consistent with the ABPP model. Think about your competence in each area and use this to highlight your strengths and your areas for improvement.

CURRENT COMPETENCY AREAS	
Science Base and Application	Individual Interactions
Assessment	Individual and Cultural Diversity
Intervention	Ethical and Legal Foundations
Consultation	Professional Identification
Supervision/Teaching (if applicable)	

PROPOSED COMPETENCY AREAS

Foundational Competencies

Professionalism (and values)—Professional values and ethics as evidenced in behavior and comportment that reflect the values and ethics of psychology, integrity, and responsibility (sub-areas include integrity, deportment, accountability, concern for the welfare of others, and professional identity).

Reflective practice, self-assessment, and self-care—Practice conducted with personal and professional self-awareness and reflection; with awareness of competencies; with appropriate self-care.

Scientific knowledge and methods—Understanding of research, research methodology, techniques of data collection and analysis, biological bases of behavior, cognitive-affective bases of behavior, and development across the lifespan. Respect for scientifically derived knowledge.

Relationships (at all levels)—Relate effectively and meaningfully with individuals, groups, and/or communities.

Individual and cultural diversity—Awareness, sensitivity, and skills in working professionally with diverse individuals, groups, and communities who represent various cultural and personal backgrounds and characteristics defined broadly and consistent with APA policy.

Ethical and legal standards—Application of ethical concepts and awareness of legal issues regarding professional activities with individuals, groups, and organizations (knowledge of ethical, legal, and professional standards and guidelines; awareness and application of ethical decision making; ethical conduct).

Interdisciplinary systems and work—Knowledge of key issues and concepts in related disciplines. Identify and interact with professionals in multiple disciplines (knowledge of the shared and distinctive contributions of other professions; functioning in multidisciplinary and interdisciplinary contexts; understanding of how participation in interdisciplinary collaboration/consultation enhances outcomes; respectful and productive relationships with individuals from other professions).

Functional Competencies

Assessment—Assessment and diagnosis of problems, capabilities, and issues associated with individuals, groups, and/or organizations.

Intervention—Interventions designed to alleviate suffering and to promote health and well-being of individuals, groups, and/or organizations (knowledge of interventions, intervention planning, skills, intervention implementation, and progress evaluation).

Consultation—The ability to provide expert guidance or professional assistance in response to a client's needs or goals (role of consultant, addressing referral question, communication of findings, application of methods).

Research and evaluation—Generating research that contributes to the professional knowledge base and/or evaluates the effectiveness of various professional activities.

Supervision—Supervision and training in the professional knowledge base and of evaluation of the effectiveness of various professional activities (expectation and roles, processes and procedures, skills development, awareness of factors affecting quality, participation in supervision process, ethical and legal issues).

Teaching—Providing instruction, disseminating knowledge, and evaluating acquisition of knowledge and skill in professional psychology.

Management and administration—Manage the direct delivery of services (DDS) and/or the administration of organizations, programs, or agencies (OPA) (management, administration, leadership, and evaluation of management and leadership).

Advocacy—Actions targeting the impact of social, political, economic, or cultural factors to promote change at the individual (client), institutional, and/or systems level (empowerment, systems change).

To persist in pursuit of Board Certification and to get the most out of it, it is essential to deal with any fears of failure and humiliation that you have regarding the exams. Otherwise, all of your efforts will be tense and tinged with those fears of being "seen" as inadequate or not good enough. If you have not had the benefit of using observed or taped sessions in supervision during your training, you might desensitize yourself to the terrors of being observed by becoming part of a peer consultation group or showing some session tapes to a trusted peer or supervisor. What this will almost certainly show you is that you really are a psychologist and not an imposter or fraud, and that you are imperfect.

Interns are often quite upset initially in internships in which their skills are objectively evaluated (which means that most of them are "average"), since they have been trained that's it's important to get all "A's," in the false culture of school grades. However, improvement requires that imperfections be recognized, and we should all get used to the fact that we are not as good at certain things (confrontation, tolerating silence, accepting "bad" behaviors on the part of clients, terminating clients who don't pay, tolerating clients who are "different" from us) as we "should" be in order to be maximally helpful.

Seeing yourself for who you are as a psychologist, who you are in terms of the personal qualities that are important for your work, and coming to accept the realization you will tame your fears of being observed. The examiners know that you aren't perfect, and you will make the best impression if you recognize your imperfections, are able to keep these issues from reducing the quality of your services to clients, and have plans to improve. Accepting your knowledge and skills as they actually are is the biggest challenge, though, and if you can do that with some equanimity, you will tolerate and benefit from the exam process.

It is important to believe in yourself in regard to the exam, and this is reasonable to do, since the standard is only somewhat higher than what we expect for licensure. Just by being licensed, you are already "in the ballpark" and are likely to pass. Finally, praise and appreciate yourself for having the desire to pass the highest level exam the profession has to offer and become Board Certified. You are exactly the kind of psychologist that we want to become Board Certified!

SETTING REALISTIC TIMELINES

There are two considerations with regard to timelines. The procedures of ABCP specify that the Practice Samples must be submitted within one year after your application is accepted (with the data collected within 6 months of submission). The other factor is your own ability to devote time to the process. Most applicants take between a year and a year and a half to go from application to oral exam, but if you can readily decide what Practice Samples to submit and easily do the videos, the total time can be somewhat less. The greatest personal factors that lengthen the total process time are indecision and reluctance to actually do the recordings. The greatest organizational factor that lengthens the total process time is scheduling the oral.

Once you pass Stage II of the process, you have some choice in how much time you want to have before the oral (for preparation). See

Chapter 5 to get a sense of how much oral exam preparation you might want to do. Between 2 and 6 months should be quite sufficient.

OBTAINING A MENTOR

For many people, having a mentor during the exam process is helpful. It is certainly not essential to interact with a mentor, but if you would like to have someone knowledgeable about the process of whom to ask questions or seek opinions, then you can obtain a mentor.

The American Academy of Clinical Psychology (AACP) offers mentors—just e-mail contact@aacpsy.org to start the process. These mentors will help with your questions and provide encouragement. They can help you to present yourself and your skills in a way that makes an appropriate exam outcome probable. They will probably not be near you geographically, so most contact will be by e-mail and phone. They will not review and comment on your video Practice Samples or Contextual Statements, because obviously those must be your work alone since you are the one seeking Board Certification. Members of APA Division 42 who are applying for the Senior Option can also obtain a mentor through the Division's new mentoring program.

You can also seek a mentor yourself from among the 1,300 or so active Board Certified Clinical Psychologists across the country. You can ask senior psychologists you know for suggestions on whom to contact, and you can search the directories in www.abpp.org and www.aacpsy.org for Board Certified Clinical Psychologists in your area and approach them directly.

WORKING WITH A GROUP TO PREPARE

It can be quite useful to work with another person or a group as you prepare, particularly for the oral exam. Others can look at some of your regular work (reports, intakes, case notes) to help you evaluate your strengths and weaknesses. They should not, on the other hand, review or comment on the video Practice Samples or Contextual Statements that you submit, since those should be your work alone. You can also get valuable feedback from practicing with others your responses to likely questions on the oral. (See Chapter 5 to get some idea about likely questions.)

It could be helpful to share the whole journey with another candidate, all the way from commitment to oral, and if you have a colleague who is interested in Board Certification, having that shared support can be very helpful to both. Think about the psychologists that you know who are nearby, and see if any of them might join you in your Board Certification quest. Unfortunately, there is no mechanism at present for locating other people across the country who are applying at the same time that you are. However, if you do know of someone applying who is not in close proximity to you, you could still prepare together by utilizing internet conferencing.

INFORMATION FOR STUDENTS

By reading the application criteria early, students can plan their training to ensure it will qualify for Board Certification. Most especially, this means making sure that you have the required year (or years) of post-doctoral experience supervised specifically by a licensed psychologist (in addition to the internship year that included supervision by a licensed psychologist). If you attend a formal post-doctoral program, this will be automatic, but if you do not, then be sure that you have at least one of your qualifying post-doctoral years required for application supervised by a licensed psychologist.

Students may now start the process of applying while still in graduate school, through ABPP's Early Entry Program. This allows you to begin banking your credentials as you complete them (doctorate, internship, post-doc), for only $25 (a $100 savings on the application fee) and to submit your application and Practice Samples before you are licensed (you must be licensed to take the exam). Some graduate schools are paying the $25 fee for any student who applies. See "Early Entry Option" on the homepage of www.abpp.org for more information.

OTHER RESOURCES

More information about ABPP Board Certification is available, of course, on www.abpp.org and on the website of the AACP, www.aacpsy.org. A recent book edited by Dr. Christine Maguth Nezu,

Dr. A. J. Finch, and Dr. Norma Simon (2009), *Becoming Board Certified by the American Board of Professional Psychology*, published by Oxford University Press, with ABPP's imprimatur, speaks to various aspects of Board Certification in general (while this present book addresses Board Certification in Clinical Psychology specifically). You can gain information and insights about ABPP itself and its governance and activities through perusing issues of "The Specialist," ABPP's journal for Board Certified psychologists, which is posted on the website.

TIPS FOR SUCCESS

- Consider thoughtfully and identify your motives (personal and professional goals and standards, concrete benefits, pay raise, etc.), which will help you to stay focused on your goal.
- Approach the whole process as a rather large learning experience. There is much to be gained in self-knowledge, and this will show you areas in which it would be good for you to gain more knowledge and skill.
- View your knowledge and skills realistically, but still know that you are a qualified psychologist.
- Deal with your fears of failure and humiliation. Find an attitude that allows you to display your sense of positivity and hope.
- Get a mentor, if you want. Mentors are available, helpful, and undemanding.
- Fill out all forms accurately and completely. Make sure that your CV is up to date. Any ambiguities may delay your advancement to candidacy.
- Be up-front about yourself in your Professional Statement. Don't make the examiners wonder who you are as a professional or wonder why that is not clear in your Professional Statement.
- Describe in your Professional Statement an ethical dilemma that was actually a dilemma and not a situation in which the "right answer" is obvious. The point is not that you knew the right thing to do, but that you used a mature and reasoned process in deciding between various priorities and options in a more complex situation.

■ Practice and get comfortable with the notion of using self-reflection to self-assess and make changes in your procedures and/or seek additional knowledge and skill. Be able to tell the examiners about your weaknesses accurately and straightforwardly, as well as how you adjust around them or have plans for improvement.

■ Choose Practice Samples carefully. Choose samples that will show typical aspects of your practice, but also ones in which you can take pride. (Be sure that the clients are comfortable with the taping and exposure.)

■ Make decent recordings. Few things are more troublesome than Practice Samples that the examiners cannot hear or samples in which they cannot see both you and the client.

■ Start the process of making the recordings and the accompanying write-ups even if you would prefer to put it off for a while. The greatest delays in the process come from candidates putting things off (since the Practice Samples are a bit of a hassle for most of us and since seeing the results makes seeing our imperfection unavoidable).

■ Demonstrate in all of your writing and speaking during the total process how your knowledge, attitudes, and actions illustrate your high standards for your professional work, rather than trying to justify your actions.

■ Write your Contextual Statements for the video Practice Samples in such a way that they clearly explain how what you did (and do) makes sense in terms of your framework of understanding human behavior and behavior change, since this is what the examiners will be most interested in. Think about this again when you review your samples and Contextual Statements before the oral.

■ Understand and represent to the examiners your attitude with regard to diversity as being truly inclusive (that your understanding of people is universal and not divided into separate understandings of "those like me" and "those not like me").

■ Be both appropriately humble and appropriately assertive in the oral.

■ Identify, before the oral, the chief challenges that you see facing the profession and decide how you think they should best be met.

■ Approach the process believing that you are appropriate for Board Certification. In the various parts of the process, illustrate why that is true.

IT ALL BEGINS WITH THE APPLICATION

Now that you have made the commitment to become Board Certified, there's no time like the present to demonstrate your commitment concretely by completing the application, and this will also stamp your entire process with the attitude of not putting off the next step! There is no downside to getting your application in at once and passing Stage I—the Credentialing Process. This process establishes you as a candidate for further examination and verifies the necessary academic preparation, supervised experience, and professional standing required by the specialty of Clinical Psychology. Completing the application, which requires minimal expenditure of time and effort, begins the process, and completing it allows you to focus on the more time-intensive Practice Samples (Stage II).

The application process is completed online at the ABPP website, www.abpp.org. Once on the website, you will find links to apply. The generic (ABPP) application is completed by applicants for all specialty areas and can be completed online. When you select Clinical Psychology as your specialty area, you will be directed to the Specialty-Specific (Clinical Psychology) Application Form. You will also be able to complete this fillable form online, save it to your computer, and upload it with your generic application when complete. This part of the application ascertains that you meet the criteria for application for the Clinical Psychology specialty area. In addition to the generic criteria (which must be met by applicants in every specialty), applicants for Board Certification in Clinical Psychology must meet the following criteria:

- *An approved internship;*
- *Two years of post-doctoral supervision in Clinical Psychology, at least one of which was supervised by a licensed psychologist, OR a one-year accredited (APA, CPA) or approved (APPIC) post-doctoral residency training program in Clinical Psychology;*
- *Education and training preparation in Clinical Psychology that meets APA accreditation requirements.*

If you are applying for Board Certification in Clinical Psychology and your internship program was not accredited by APA or CPA and was not a member of APPIC at the time of your internship, you will need to provide a full description of your internship in your application.

Be sure to include, among other items, your title, the number of interns in the program, your clinical rotations, competencies achieved, didactic experiences, number and names of supervisors, number of hours of weekly individual supervision, number of hours of weekly group supervision, whether or not you received compensation, and the name of the Director of Internship Training.

For your post-doctoral experience and supervision, if you completed a formal post-doctoral program that was accredited by APA or CPA or was an APPIC member, provide a description of the residency program, providing the program name, program director's name, names of supervisors, and the nature of the supervised practice.

If you did not complete a formal post-doctoral program, you will need to document two years of post-doctoral experience in which at least one of the years was appropriately supervised (by a licensed psychologist). (One "year" is equivalent to 1,500 practice hours over a 12-month period.) Applicants not having completed a formal training program should be certain that the reviewers have sufficient information to evaluate the experience by providing detailed dates, hours, names of agencies/practices, nature of the work performed, the supervisory arrangements, your supervisors' names, your title at the time of being a supervisee, and the nature of the supervised practice.

Both the Specialty Application Form and the online generic application are required for your application to be complete. After having completed the Specialty Form and saving it to upload at a later time, you will be ready to complete the generic online application. This section is related to the generic requirements for Board Certification (basic ABPP requirements that apply to applicants of all fifteen specialty boards).

The generic requirements are that an individual has completed a doctoral degree from a program in professional psychology that was accredited by the APA or the Canadian Psychological Association (CPA), or was listed by the Association of State and Provincial Psychology Boards (ASPPB). There are exceptions to this requirement for graduates from programs prior to 1983. These applicants may request that their education and training credentials be reviewed individually to determine ABPP eligibility.

In addition to the generic doctoral degree requirement there is a generic internship requirement. Documentation of internships on graduate school transcripts varies greatly from program to program. Thus, for both generic and specialty requirements, you will need to have documentation beyond that evidenced on your transcript, such as a letter of completion or a certificate attesting to your completion of an internship.

If you are an applicant who completed a degree prior to 1983, it would be helpful for you to support your application with other credentialing documents. If you have a Certificate of Professional Qualification (CPQ), as offered by the Association of State and Provincial Psychology Boards (ASPPB), this would suffice for the *generic* ABPP requirement. Individuals who are listed in the National Register of Health Service Providers in Psychology (NRHSPP) or the Canadian Register of Health Service Providers in Psychology (CRHSPP) may also likely be able to document the ABPP generic criteria by means of these credentials.

Licensure is also part of the generic criteria, and applicants must be licensed at the doctoral level for the independent practice of psychology. Licensure must be non-conditional and provide the professional with the unrestricted practice of psychology in the state in which he or she is licensed. Applicants who are licensed but have a history of disciplinary or ethical action must provide detailed documentation of the events for review.

The Clinical specialty's requirement for post-doctoral experience is one year completed through a formal post-doctoral program. Post-doctoral experience that was not part of a formal post-doctoral program may also qualify, but the minimum required is two years, one of which must be supervised.

Upload your generic and specialty applications, send a copy of your license and internship certificate to ABPP Central Office, and have your doctoral transcript sent directly from the institution to the Central Office of ABPP. Along with your application, send the non-refundable application fee of $125.00 to the American Board of Professional Psychology, 600 Market Street, Suite 300, Chapel Hill, NC 27516.

Once you have submitted your applications and your license to practice, your doctoral degree, program, and licensure will be verified by ABPP Central Office. You will be notified relatively quickly of the review results, and if you have met both the generic and Clinical Psychology criteria you will be eligible to proceed. Chapters 3 and 4 discuss

Stage II—Practice Samples. As soon as you send in your application, begin thinking about your Practice Samples, so that when you receive your results for Stage I, you will be ready to start work on your Professional Statement, video samples, and Contextual Statements.

REFERENCES

American Board of Clinical Psychology. (2011). *Examination manual for board certification in clinical psychology for the American board of professional psychology.* Retrieved from www.abpp.org/files/page-specific/3355%20Clinical/15_ABCP_Exam_Manual.pdf

Fouad, N. A., Grus, C. L., Hatcher, R. L., Kaslow, N. J., Hutchings, P. S., Madson, M., … Crossman, R. E. (2009). Competency benchmarks: A model for the understanding and measuring of competence in professional psychology across training levels. *Training and Education in Professional Psychology, 3,* S5–S26.

Nezu, C. M., Finch, A. J., Jr., & Simon, N. P. (Eds.). (2009). *Becoming board certified by the American Board of Professional Psychology.* New York, NY: Oxford.

THREE

Stage II: Practice Samples—The Professional Statement and Curriculum Vitae

Stage II of the Clinical ABPP application process is commonly referred to as the "Practice Samples." Because this stage of the process is perhaps the most detailed and time-consuming one for the applicant, we discuss it across two chapters in this book. This chapter covers the preparation of the Curriculum Vitae (CV) and the Professional Statement. The following chapter entitled, Stage II: Recorded Practice Samples Focusing on Assessment and Intervention, describes video recording of Practice Samples and how to proceed if the Practice Samples do not pass.

Stage II is quite different from Stage I, which is primarily documentation of your credentials. There is little latitude in Stage I to emphasize strengths or acknowledge weaknesses in the information conveyed since it is primarily factual and historical. Stage II is perhaps the stage where you, the applicant, have the best opportunity to display your knowledge and skills in a detailed fashion. The primary constraints in Stage II relate to your ability to clearly and concisely document strengths and accomplishments as they pertain to the individual areas represented in the Practice Samples.

While Stage III also serves as an opportunity to display your knowledge and skills, its format as an oral examination (although preparation will assist you in how well you do), will not permit the time for you to consider your responses in depth or perhaps otherwise identify the depth and breadth of your knowledge without the pressures of time during the exam. A well-written Practice Sample will move you a long way toward success in Stage III of the examination process. Alternatively, a marginal but passing Practice Sample will increase your burden during Stage III.

Stage II will always require a copy of your CV and a Professional Statement. The Professional Statement is limited to approximately 10 typewritten double-spaced pages covering seven specific areas in separately identified sections. Most applicants will also have to complete two separate and distinct video samples from among the four competency domains of assessment, intervention, consultation, and supervision. These will be referred to as "the video-recorded Practice Samples." The video-recorded Practice Samples will be accompanied by a written Contextual Statement, each between 1,000 and 1,500 words as well as other supporting materials including unsigned examples of releases of information and HIPAA documentation. The video-recorded Practice Samples, covered in the next chapter, must have been recorded within 6 months of their submission to the examining committee. Those seeking certification under the Senior Option may be submitting pertinent materials such as publications, brochures, or presentations from among the four competency domains in lieu of "the video-recorded Practice Samples."

Well-written and clearly communicated Professional Statements, Contextual Statements, and CV convey to the examiners your motivation and attention to detail. Your use of written language to communicate and convey an understanding of the limits of your knowledge and skills is an important determinant in how the examining committee views you. The examining committee is sensitive to cultural and ethnic diversity and will always consider this in reviewing written and oral materials. However, careless use of punctuation or grammar, spelling errors, and errors due to not reading instructions carefully do not reflect well upon the examinee's efforts. Be sure to rely upon a careful reading of the documents rather than solely a careful electronic spell checking of the document.

The American Academy of Clinical Psychologists (AACP) is a membership organization that represents ABPP Board Certified Clinical Psychologists, and its board has developed and adopted guidelines concerning the role of formal mentors with regard to reading, editing, or guiding the application process. We can informally identify three types of assistants or mentors the candidate may utilize: (a) AACP formally recognize mentors (Appendix A,www.aacpsy.org), (b) lay mentors with no formal recognition that are generally friends (readers without professional expertise in the areas covered) but who may be helpful in terms of clarity of communication, grammar, and the nontechnical aspects of writing, and (c) collegial mentors not formally recognized but readers who may have similar backgrounds and expertise in the areas being covered by the Practice Sample and therefore may be able to advise the applicant to develop the area more. AACP mentors will be Board Certified in the area of specialty (i.e., Clinical Psychology) and will adhere to the guidelines for mentoring approved in 2012. Collegial mentors may be, but are not necessarily, Board Certified; nor are they necessarily Board Certified in the area of specialization for which you may be seeking Board Certification. AACP-approved mentors may be very valuable in assisting you in the certification process both through knowledge and support. However, ultimately the candidate retains responsibility for following the application procedures and should not rely upon the mentor for anything other than support and assistance. For technical concerns, the applicant/candidate should rely upon the resources provided by the AACP and by the American Board of Clinical Psychology (ABCP).

Mentors are not required in order to seek and succeed at earning Clinical Specialty Board Certification, although many candidates find their mentorships valuable. Generally mentors should assist with general advice and comments. They should not be involved in improving any specifics within the Practice Sample with a goal of making the candidate "look better." They may only assist in helping the candidate be a better candidate. The psychologist may have more than one mentor, although only one AACP mentor is permitted at a time. This practice of having multiple mentors is neither encouraged nor discouraged. Ultimately the mentee may decide upon the need for a mentor(s) based upon availability and the mentee's perceived strengths and weaknesses. Certainly, more mentors increase the risk of contradictory information or recommendations. The mentee will need to decide upon which advice to follow.

Whether completing Stage II under the Senior Option or the traditional application path, please remember that all submissions in

Stage II are in triplicate. This would include video recordings, CV, and any other submitted materials. Video recordings may be submitted by thumb drive (USB solid-state memory device) or DVD. Blank copies of any informed consent forms that you use in addition to the blank ABPP consent forms required for the videotaping should be included. In addition you will need to include copies of your Health Insurance Portability and Accountability Act (HIPAA) information documents and, again, only unsigned documents are acceptable. While ABCP is considering the possibility of submitting the Professional Statement and other documentation in electronic format, that option is not presently available. If this is a desirable option for you, then you may wish to contact ABCP to see if their policy has changed when you are ready to submit your materials.

THE CURRICULUM VITAE (REQUIRED OF ALL APPLICANTS)

The CV is an important supporting document to your clinical board application, and should be reviewed in detail before submission. Failing to provide a broad and comprehensive CV may inadvertently make successful completion of Stage II more difficult. It is increasingly common for individuals to customize their CVs in support of a position, job, or activity they are seeking. You might not be well served by providing such a CV if you were overly narrow in describing your experience. For example, while it might not be important to acknowledge work with the severely mentally ill when applying for a position as an Employee Assistance Plan counselor, you would not want to fail to acknowledge such experience in support of your Board Certification. Remember that the clinical boards represent broad knowledge of Clinical Psychology and not narrow or specific expertise alone. Unlike the CV you might customarily be using for employment purposes, which may be more narrowly focused, you might want to take the opportunity to revise your CV with an eye toward identifying both the breadth and depth of your experience in your clinical field.

If you are early in your career or have not had much opportunity to submit your CV, you may want to review it with particular sensitivity to the transition from student to professional. Generally, you will not want to provide detailed information about your practicum placements, teaching assistant positions, and other work leading up to your terminal degree. It is presumed that upon having reached your terminal degree and becoming licensed that you had reasonably appropriate educational and work experiences leading up to your terminal degree. In this regard, the CV will most likely look very different from the one you would have submitted in support of seeking pre-doctoral internship or postdoctoral training. Early career psychologists, psychologists that have been working in a narrow area of employment or with only one employer, may have a more brief experience history than a later career psychologist or someone in a small practice working in many areas. The examining committee anticipates this so it is expected that the length of a CV is not a good measure of the clinician's knowledge and skills. Avoid the temptation to use a whole page to describe a single experience with a limited population.

Unrelated work experiences or professions such as working in fast food restaurants, or as an automotive mechanic, plumber, or nanny are not generally considered relevant to your professional psychology work. These work experiences need not be included in your CV. However, if your current work in the field is somehow directly related to previous employment experiences, you may want to identify those in your pre-doctoral experience. For example, if a significant portion of your psychotherapy service is in the specialized area of working with school teachers, and you had previously been a school teacher before obtaining your doctorate in psychology, you may well want to include that in your CV. The CV is not a resume covering all of your employment history. It is a document focused on your professional work as a psychologist. It should be focused on psychology service in support of your work within your area of psychology.

It is often helpful to have a colleague or mentor review your CV. It is surprising what others catch that you may not notice. A common point of confusion that might be caught by reading with fresh eyes is for a psychologist to "clearly label" headings within the CV, which may seem perfectly clear to the applicant but may be confusing to other readers. For example, the heading "presentations" might appear to convey that the psychologist made the following presentations. However, the psychologist may have meant that these were presentations he had attended. Similarly, "training" might represent postdoctoral training that the psychologist received rather than that he provided. It is certainly appropriate to identify specialized training or supervision that you have, but it should not be a struggle for the reviewer to figure out whether this is supervision or training that you provided rather than received. Generally, continuing education services that you receive but do not lead to a specific certification or credentialing would not be identified in the CV. Presentations, awards, service, and elective offices should be placed on your CV. Citing presentations or training using American Psychological Association (APA) format, since it includes the name of the presenter, readily differentiates training or presentations that you provide from those that have been provided to you.

While we generally recommend that individuals look through some of the various websites devoted to writing a CV, we would also encourage some caution. Many of these websites are designed for professionals seeking employment. As such, they recommend providing a personal history such as date of birth, marital status, number of children, favorite activities, et cetera. While this may be appropriate for a business resume, this information is generally thought to be extraneous for a professional CV and particularly with regard to consideration for Board Certification in psychology. Accordingly, we would not recommend including such information. Similarly, and again more appropriate to resume writing, these sites may recommend placing bullet points describing what you believe to be your best assets. This might include such things as "energetic," "self-starter," etc. Just as personal information may not be relevant to Board Certification, eye-catching bullet points may be seen as a distraction in reviewing your CV.

We would also caution you in the use of the term "expert." Too often in an attempt to impress future employers an individual's CV will summarize their skills as being expert in 10 or more things. Undoubtedly, there are a few psychologists who are validly expert in 10 or more things within psychology, but there are relatively few psychologists, particularly early in their career, that can validly claim expertise in so many things. Claiming such expertise will probably elicit inquiry by the examiners. It would be important to make sure that your level of expertise is expert relative to most psychologists rather than expert compared to the lay public.

While it is important to convey your achievements and accomplishments as a psychologist thus far in your career, you may wish to be sensitive to the inclusion of things that may represent exaggeration or perhaps come across as exaggeration even if they are not. For example, there are CVs indicating that the professional graduated cum laude or summa cum laude from his graduate program. While such meritorious academic achievements are noteworthy, they are almost exclusively awarded at the undergraduate level and seldom if ever at the graduate level of training in colleges within the United States. Graduate schools do not generally award distinctions for meritorious academic achievement. Accordingly, claiming graduation as a cum laude or summa cum laude from the graduate program is likely to increase scrutiny.

Similarly, one should be careful in labeling academic credentials. Do not list, for example, "graduate of Harvard University" if you graduated from a non-credit internet extension course for Harvard University. It is certainly appropriate to acknowledge completion of some type of program from a renowned university's (or any university's) extension curriculum, but it is not a fair characterization of your achievement to suggest the completion of a brief and non-competitive non-credit course or training is the equivalent of completion of a course of training in a degree-granting institution's course of study. It may, at the least, elicit questions as to how competitive the degree or certification was and what type of distinction it would make if it was not competitive. Similar concerns are raised by individuals that have vanity credentials. We are all familiar with certifying bodies that grant certification based solely upon the payment of a fee. Citing one or more of these credentials will not be seen as enhancing your professional credibility by the examining committee.

Having covered the many things that you may want to avoid writing or revising in your CV, we will now address the many things that should be included. Anything that you have done in support of the profession should be included in your CV. This is important whether it is speaking to mosques, synagogues, churches, civic organizations, or any other groups about psychological issues and concerns. Similarly, television, radio, or newspaper pieces, or blogs that you have provided or to which you have contributed as related to professional psychology should be reflected. If you have been active in promoting psychology to politicians either through lobbying or some other form of action, this too would be important to mention. While contributions to psychological political action committees are welcomed, more direct action in the form of lobbying, fund raising, or speaking to organizations about psychology, psychology's function, or even political issues affecting psychology are important to include. Promotion of the profession is viewed favorably.

While psychologists' training histories should be more similar than different by the time they attain their doctorates, employment activities are presumed to be much more diverse. Accordingly, it is important for you to detail the kinds of activities you engage in and specialized areas of concentration in your work. These may not be large areas of practice but are areas in which you have developed greater expertise.

Contributions in the form of committee work or leadership to state, local, or national organizations supporting psychology should always be noted. If you have served on committees for a psychological association, or been elected or appointed as an officer in psychological organizations, these too should be identified. Volunteer work or board membership for organizations like CHADD (Children and Adults with Attention Deficit/Hyperactivity Disorder) or NAMI (National Alliance on Mentally Illness) should be identified. In general, you are better served by having been a member of one or more psychologically based organizations than not being in such an association. Such associations are believed to further the practitioner's knowledge of psychology, the psychological community in the area, and generally contribute to being a more diversified and knowledgeable psychologist.

Certainly, if you have published research, scholarly papers, presentations to psychologists, guest lecturing, or other more academic endeavors, it is important to identify these in your CV. Educating fellow professionals, including supervision of other professionals, should always be identified.

Comments on the Fictional Curriculum Vitae

Exhibit 3.1 is a fictional CV that, although much abbreviated, may not be particularly unusual for an early career psychologist. Unless the early career psychologist has significant publications and presentations from his training program and internship, it is unlikely that he would have started into a new practice and still had an opportunity to get his

Exhibit 3.1
Fictional Curriculum Vitae Sample (with comments in italics)

NAME

Jonathan "John" Doe, Psy. D.

1 First Avenue North

Some City, State XXXXX

DrJohnDoe@JOHNDOE.Com

Telephone: 1(800) xxx-xxxx

PERSONAL HISTORY

Married twice

Three children: one boy and two girls. Ages 4 to 9

Caretaker for elderly mother

While all of these accomplishments are interesting and provide details about Dr. Doe, they are generally not believed to be relevant to a professional CV. The personal history section is more common in a job resume than a CV and may not be needed in a CV. If there is some particular relevance of the personal history it might be appropriate to the CV. For example, nationality might be relevant, bilingualism, missionary services, or military service might be relevant experiences as they pertain to the practice of the profession.

EDUCATION

Doctor of Philosophy awarded summa cum laude by State University, 2005

Notice inconsistency between degree awarded and signature line (i.e., does Dr. Doe have a PhD in psychology or a PsyD Doctorate in Psychology). Does this represent carelessness or does this individual have multiple earned doctorates? Does the applicant know the difference among the degrees? Not knowing would be a concern for the competency of professional awareness. Was this an APA-approved program? The award summa cum laude is seldom granted in Doctoral- or Masters-level programs in the United States, even if he did graduate in the top 5% of the class. This may speak to inflation of credentials or lack of professional awareness.

Pre-Doctoral Internship completed in 2005 with the University of Diversity, University City, Florida. Completed in 2005 with emphasis on behavioral health and child assessment.

(Continued)

Exhibit 3.1 (*Continued*)
Fictional Curriculum Vitae Sample (with comments in italics)

Bachelor of Arts in Psychology awarded magna cum laude by State University in 2001
It is entirely possible that this individual graduated with the award of cum laude since this was an undergraduate bachelor's level program.
Diploma awarded by Good High School in 1993
It is not customary to identify high school in a professional CV

DOCTORAL DISSERTATION

TITLE:	Prolonged exposure in combat-exposed female veterans
DIRECTOR:	Another Doctor, PhD

EMPLOYMENT
2006 to Present
I am currently a contract employee for the U.S. Army base in Houston Texas. In this capacity I serve the enlisted members and officers' psychological needs. Specifically I am one of six psychologists providing short-term psychotherapy services lasting approximately three 1-hour contacts. The most commonly addressed problems are relationship problems, problems with finances, alcohol abuse, and major depression. One day a week I provide telephone on-call services to the medics and physicians as a consultant.
The writer might have been better served by choosing different words or explaining better regarding the 1-hour contacts. It is difficult to imagine what kind of psychotherapy could take place in three 1-hour contacts, particularly given that some type of data gathering and history taking must take place. This may be a workable and appropriate model but the wording leads to questions about the parameters.

2005 to 2006
I completed 1 year of supervised postdoctoral training at a community mental health center in Anchorage Alaska. In this capacity the majority of my populations served were the indigenous

peoples of Alaska and approximately 10% of my population served was non-native Alaskans. Services were wide-ranging including chronic depression, panic disorders, and personality disorders.

This is a fairly brief description of this training that might benefit from elaboration on the number of supervisors and whether there were formal rotations. However, the examinee will have ample opportunity to expound upon the services provided in this placement in the professional work section of their Professional Statement.

PUBLICATIONS, PAPERS, AND PRESENTATIONS

Larry & John, Responsible Psychological Practice, Lawrenceville Mental Health Gathering, Lawrenceville Alaska, June 23, 2012.

Based solely upon the citation format this is believed to be something that Dr. Doe attended rather than presented. Generally, attendances at symposia or presentations are not cited in CV.

Doe, Smith, and Doe, Risk Management and Liability, Lucyville Hospital, May 13, 2010.

This appears to be a professional presentation provided by Dr. Doe. This would be an appropriate use of the citation.

Doe, J., Why should we support Mr. Smith as our congressmen? Lucyville Herald Tribune and Post, Editorial November, 2010.

On the face of it this appears to be an editorial in a local news-paper about someone that is running for office. Ordinarily, such editorial comments would not be placed in among scholarly works. Conceivably, if this were entirely related to mental health issues and therefore represented some type of public education it might be appropriate. However, on the face of it this would seem to be an attempt to fatten up Dr. Doe's accomplishments.

ELECTIVE OFFICES, AWARDS, SERVICE, AND HONORS

2010 to present: Membership chair, Libertarians of Lucyville
1993:   Good High School Prom King

While these represent legitimate accomplishments that Dr. Doe should rightfully feel proud of, they are largely irrelevant to his profession as a psychologist. Accordingly they need not appear in his professional CV.

(Continued)

Exhibit 3.1 (*Continued*)

Fictional Curriculum Vitae Sample (with comments in italics)

PROFESSIONAL AND SCIENTIFIC AFFILIATIONS

Member:	Alaska Psychological Association.
Staff:	Fort Hospital, MEDCOM Fort Hospital, U.S. Army Base Houston, Texas

These would seem to be appropriate professional affiliations demonstrating some connection to the profession of psychology.

---

post-training life in order to begin to build a research history, publications, and presentations. Therefore, while this is a shorter CV than might be expected of a more senior clinician, it does serve to identify some strengths and weaknesses in CV writing. It is important for the CV to convey to the reader the professional's accomplishments. As has been identified, some of the entries are confusing to the reader and do not clearly identify what the relationship is between the profession and the items cited. There is always a problem in identifying important information that should be placed in the description of an activity and making that entry so long that it will be ignored or overlooked by the reader. Fortunately, entries like presentations and publications have APA-approved citation standards. These may be relied upon so that the individual provides sufficient information that the original citation can be identified and that is generally sufficient to clarify the writer's role with regard to the citation. Additionally, the CV is not a place to add personal information, political views, or even continuing education unless it is identified by the presence of some type of certification.

THE PROFESSIONAL STATEMENT (REQUIRED OF ALL APPLICANTS)

In beginning the Professional Statement you should plan around the 10-page, double-spaced page limit covering the seven areas required. The areas are: Professional Work; Science Base and Application; Assessment,

Intervention, Teaching, Supervision; Discussion of Complex Professional Relations; Examples of Specific Diversity-Related Issues; Ethics Example; and Ethical and Legal Status. There is some latitude allowed in the 10 pages but generally you would not want the Professional Statement to exceed 10 pages by more than a page. Fewer pages are acceptable but you would not want to sacrifice detail and clarity to save pages. While 10 pages double-spaced may sound like a lot of material, with seven areas to cover it is surprisingly easy to run out of space. Most people find that they need more rather than fewer pages.

While the Professional Statement is considered one document, it is split into seven separate and distinct sections, each of which should be labeled and identifiable as such. Since each of these areas is separate and distinct you should be careful not to make the mistake of using the same example in multiple areas. For example, while the description of your complex interpersonal interaction may involve diversity issues and even ethical issues, you must use separate examples for diversity, ethics, and for a complex interaction. While it is appropriate to comment on diversity issues and ethical issues or complex interactions in each section, they cannot be combined into one example satisfying all three areas. Remember to use proper APA format for any citations or references. In preparing the Professional Statement it would be helpful to familiarize yourself with and perhaps refer back to the "Example of Professional Statement" provided on the ABPP Clinical Psychology portion of the website devoted to the application process. There will also be some examples with commentary provided with the descriptions below.

In reading the descriptions below it is important to keep in mind that the examining committee does not score each area within the Professional Statement individually, nor is the work sample scored separately. The examining committee reviews the entire Professional Statement (i.e., all seven areas contained in the 10 pages), your CV, and the video recordings before scoring the examinee in the competency areas. The Examining committee is responsible for assessing nine identified areas of Competency. The Competency areas scored are: Science Base and Application; Assessment; Intervention; Consultation; Supervision/Teaching; Interpersonal Interactions; Individual and Cultural Diversity; Ethics and Legal Foundations; and Professional

Identification. Some areas in the Professional Statement may not speak to a competency area, while other areas may contain information that is scorable in more than one competency area. In this regard, the Professional Statement's sections do not correspond directly and singularly with the competency areas scored by the examiner.

To clarify, let's use as an example the competency of Ethics and Legal Foundations. In the Professional Statement, "Professional Work" may not provide any information that allows the examiner to determine competency of Ethics and Legal Foundations. However, the examiner looks at all seven areas of the materials (i.e., Professional Work; Science Base and Application; Assessment, Intervention, Teaching, Supervision; Discussion of Complex Professional Relations; Examples of Specific Diversity-Related Issues; Ethics Example; and Ethical and Legal Status) as well as the CV, and the video recordings and assigns an overall competency of Ethics and Legal Foundations score. So if other areas of the Professional Statement displayed acceptable Ethics and Legal Foundations, then this area of competency would be scored as passed. This is significant because it also means that an examinee might have a very good "Ethics Example" in her Professional Statement but displayed substandard ethics in the "Discussion of Complex Professional Relations" and in the video recordings, potentially resulting in a failure of the competency of Ethics and Legal Foundations. The competency areas are evaluated continuously across the Professional Statement (i.e., all seven areas), the work samples, and CV, and not simply one area (i.e., without regard to the label of the area) within the submitted material.

In all of the following fictitious examples a "Better" and a "More Problematic" example are given. It is important to keep in mind that the examining committee reviews the entire Professional Statement (i.e., all seven areas contained in the 10 pages), the CV, and the video recordings of the Practice Samples before scoring the examinee in the competency areas for Stage II. Accordingly, it is possible that apparent weaknesses identified may be competently and thoroughly addressed elsewhere in the candidate's submitted documents. The reader should not believe that "Better" examples equate to passing examples or that "More Problematic" examples equate to failing examples since the passing or failing is a combination multiple datum scored in multiple areas.

Topic 1: Professional Work

The professional work section will be somewhat redundant with portions of your CV. The primary difference is that this description of your work will be more thorough and detailed with regard to your current activities and how you complete them. You should approach this with a more narrative and descriptive style as opposed to a list of activities and achievements. To the extent possible, you should try to identify the amount of time spent in each of the activities as a percentage of time. Thus, if you complete psychological evaluations you might want to indicate that it is 25% of your time and then describe how the remaining 75% of the time is consumed in other activities. While this is not necessary, it is often helpful for the examiners in understanding your practice and practice patterns.

This section should address your current professional work. It should identify the nature of the company you are working for if you are not in independent practice. You will need to describe the nature of the work of the practice or employer as well as your specific duties and activities. Describe how you maintain currency in the profession by describing the continuing education activities in which you participate. You will need to identify both formal educational means, including reading, continuing education programs, classes that you attend, and clinical supervision, as well as informal means such as informal supervision from colleagues. Identify services and activities you provide to state, local, or national professional organizations. You will need to describe your long-term plans for your future in psychology and explain your reasons for seeking Board Certification. See the Clinical Exam Manual for the ABCP's formal statement of content requirements.

Better Professional Work Statement Example
(with comments in italics)

I completed my graduate training from a predominantly cognitive behavioral training program. In my present employment I am working in an independent practice setting with a patient population that is predominantly female (approximately 60%) and exclusively adult. The majority of my clients experience anxiety-related disorders including panic disorder, generalized anxiety disorder, and occasionally obsessive-compulsive disorder. The remainder of my client population, which is probably 40%, represents mood disorders, predominantly major depression and dysthymia.

This population is particularly amenable to cognitive behavioral interventions, and I rely upon evidence-based treatment where such evidenced-based therapy exists. I maintain a close relationship with a few colleagues from graduate school also practicing in town. One is a neuropsychologist whom I rely upon for information and cross refer with. The other colleague is predominantly a family therapist and we occasionally cross refer. We have formed a professional support group; we meet to talk about practice issues and to discuss our cases. We meet once a week, and occasionally when we do not have practice issues or specific therapy issues to address we will bring articles for discussion.

I am currently working to establish a consulting relationship with the local community mental health center that does not have any doctoral-level therapists. I agreed to provide free supervision 1 hour a week for 3 months. At that time we will try to establish a financial contract.

I am seeking Board Certification because I believe it represents the future of psychology. That is, just like medicine, psychologists increasingly narrow their scope of practice, hone their proficiencies, and seek to identify this increased area of specialization.

Comments—This psychologist clearly identifies the client population and does so by citing the proportion of cases and the population. In this fashion the psychologist gives the reader confidence that he has thought about his population and that it is narrow enough that he can remain proficient in it. Specific modalities are linked to the population. His training was predominantly cognitive behavioral and this presumably would provide a good basis for treatment services in that area (and also begins to establish his scientific background and skill level).

The population statistics suggest that the practice does not have much ethnic or cultural diversity, although this is not clear. The psychologist is establishing relationships with other psychologists as well as establishing a support system, thus indicating the desire to maintain a strong professional identity. The candidate, however, has not included comments on his continuing education activities or his long-term plans in psychology, as required in the instructions. Notice that the psychologist speaks to the reason for seeking

Board Certification by also including observations about the profession and thereby demonstrating professional identity and sensitivity to current psychological/professional issues.

More Problematic Professional Work Statement
Example (with comments in italics)

I completed my training in a predominantly psychodynamic training program. I have found Rogerian client-centered psychotherapeutic techniques to be more appropriate for my population. My population is highly varied including schizophrenic patients, children, old people, several recent refugees, and the occasional anxiety patient. I work in a fairly economically depressed part of town and see a number of patients that have transportation problems as well as problems getting social service support for their therapy services.

I provide some consultation to the local hospital, seeing mostly oncology patients. There I have the opportunity to interface with physicians and nurses and this gives me access to a large medical library. This provides me the opportunity to look up some information or get interlibrary loans through the medical library.

I am seeking Board Certification at this time because I feel that this is a good time in my life to do so. My practice is fairly stable, my services are fairly routine, and I feel that seeking Board Certification will broaden my knowledge base by providing me an opportunity to review my cases and refresh my memory regarding the literature relevant to my services.

Comments—This psychologist provides good detail about the population being served, including a variety of types of clients. Such diversity does result, though, in an increased burden to demonstrate competence in all areas. The psychologist describes himself as trained in a psychodynamic model but working in a Rogerian model. Neither of these models provides much literature for the treatment and management of patients with schizophrenia, which this provider indicates is part of his treatment population. It is also unclear how the psychologist obtained and maintains sufficient knowledge and skill in a model that may be quite different from the one in which he is trained. Additionally, he does not describe how the Rogerian approach is more effective, how he assessed it to be more effective, and whether there is any literature to support the greater effectiveness.

The treatment population is not only diverse diagnostically, but it appears to be culturally diverse, and this is not addressed. Further, the psychologist identifies the geriatric or elderly population as "old people," which is not terribly precise and suggests some cultural insensitivity. On a positive note this psychologist is providing services in a general hospital to maintain a psychology presence there, which may show commitment to a professional identity involving service. It also provides him with an opportunity to maintain currency by accessing the medical library.

The psychologist provides a somewhat relevant statement with regard to the reason for seeking Board Certification. He does identify the need to remain current with regard to the profession and to assess his practice relative to current standards and literature, but it would be hoped that the psychologist would do this even without the motivation of Board Certification. This section of the Professional Statement does not include, as it should, continuing education activities or long-term plans in psychology.

Topic 2: Science Base and Application

You will need to describe your knowledge of the science behind Clinical Psychology as it guides your practice of the profession. In doing this you must either speak to your current clinical research activities or discuss the research basis for your professional practices and practice patterns. Descriptions of your research and methods can be summarized along with topics of your research. This will serve to convey sufficient information and demonstrate the science behind your research rather than simply identifying that you conduct research. It is recognized that many Clinical Psychologists are not involved in research.

With regard to demonstrating the scientific basis of your clinical services you should be able to identify scholarly works that serve as the basis of your treatment. Identification of scholarly works is the beginning of demonstration of the scientific basis, but some understanding of the research and science that support the treatment interventions will also be necessary. You will also need to address the means you use to determine effectiveness of your treatment services. For example, you might discuss how you measure your treatment goals in your treatment plans.

Better Science Base and Application Statement Example
(with comments in italics)

I have been very fortunate as a Clinical Psychologist by having found a community college where I have been able to teach a course on abnormal psychology. This not only allows me to contribute to the community but it also allows me an opportunity to critically review research in my profession in order to present relevant information to my students. In this way not only am I able to maintain currency in the field of Clinical Psychology but I also have the opportunity to exercise my knowledge and skill base in determining the quality of the research available in determining the value of presenting the research to my students. This also provides me the opportunity to speak to the students about psychological research methods and statistics. Although that is not the primary focus of the course, it serves as a useful venue to begin to expose them to how knowledge in the area of psychology is developed and disseminated.

A recent example of how this assists me with my practice is an article in the *Journal of Clinical Psychology* (Boo, 2011). It reviewed predictors of suicide and once again identified that black males have a lower risk of suicide than Caucasian males. While this has been found repeatedly in the past, it is good to see that we can continue to rely upon Caucasian race and male gender as a slightly greater risk factor for suicide (Coo, 2003).

Comments—The psychologist has identified a source of professional knowledge but does not state how what is learned is relevant to her practice, since that practice is not described. The psychologist establishes how she obtains and maintains knowledge of the literature. While it is only important that Board applicants demonstrate that they continue to remain current with the science of psychology, it is relevant to know that in this case the psychologist is keeping up with the science of psychology in at least one way that is presumably relevant to her practice.

A culturally/ethnically relevant issue is cited. Also note that the psychologist properly cites research articles using APA format. [These are fictitious citations and the Table of References will not be generated for these examples, but real work samples should contain citations and references for the examiners as part of the Practice Samples.] Finally, identifying that the finding of elevated suicide risk factors is not new demonstrates that the psychologist has some knowledge of the existing literature. However, the psychologist does not describe how she confirms the effectiveness of her services, which is required in the instructions.

More Problematic Science Base and Application Statement Example (with comments in italics)

My practice is primarily limited to the treatment of adults with depressive disorders. The narrow scope of my practice is helpful in reducing the number and types of resources I have to review in order to remain current. I am fortunate in that I am able to get most of my information by attending case studies in the community. These case studies are most useful because they typically involve case presentations of clients that are very similar to mine. Local experts in the community talk about the treatment of the disorder and their interventions. Other skilled clinicians are able to chime in and provide alternative explanations for the patients' behavior.

It is my goal to begin to collect some of these discussions and to summarize them with thoughts and recommendations from my colleagues. I would hope that this could be published either in the form of a book or perhaps as contributions to a journal.

Comments—The candidate has cited a single narrow evidence base and method of learning and keeping up with developments in the field. Case studies are generally thought to be among the weakest forms of the scientific method and data gathering in psychology. This psychologist indicates that the majority of his knowledge and skill comes from this modality and more significantly from this one forum. It is recognized that some psychological interventions are less amenable to more rigorous scientific inquiry, but this does not mean that the psychologist should rely only upon the weakest form of scientific evidence.

The psychologist identifies his population, which is fairly narrow, and notes that the case presentations are more similar to his population than not. The psychologist does indicate a desire to collect the case samples discussed in this forum and to disseminate them to a wider audience, thus recognizing some professional obligation to disseminate helpful professional information. He does not describe how he confirms the effectiveness of his services, which is required by the instructions.

Topic 3: Assessment, Intervention, Teaching, Supervision

You will need to discuss your current assessment approaches, your interventions or treatments, and your consultations. Discuss supervision and teaching activities if they are applicable to your services. Candidates are not required to provide such services and are not penalized if they do not.

You may want to discuss how you address an intake or referral. If you provide more formal assessment you would need to describe the techniques that you use, the frequency of use, and your preferred instruments. Link your assessment approach and results to your treatment approach or recommendations for treatment or intervention.

Describe your theoretical orientation or orientations. If your approach is eclectic you should identify three or more specific theories, schools, or approaches and describe how they guide and influence your treatment and formulation of the case. You should explain how your theoretical orientation contributes to your conceptualization of the case and informs your attitudes about the individual. You must address cultural diversity as it impacts your assessment and treatment. Similarly, when discussing supervision or consultation activities, if you engage in them, you should address the relevance of cultural diversity to those services.

(Note that the examples for this item only describe a single area of practice [i.e., assessment] out of convenience and concern for brevity. It is expected that your statement in this work sample will address all areas in which you practice from the list of: Assessment, Intervention, Teaching, and Supervision.)

Better Assessment, Intervention, Teaching, Supervision Statement Example (with comments in italics)

A significant portion of my current practice involves providing psychological assessments to aid the surgeons in the community with bariatric surgery. Specifically, I try to establish whether the individual has sufficient understanding of the surgical procedure and risks/benefits in order to provide informed consent. Part of this assessment is by direct inquiry to determine whether the individual understands the explanation provided to them and remembers the explanation provided to them about the surgery. In this context I also provide some standardized assessment instruments tailored to the inquiry. For example, for individuals who are known to have cognitive weakness or educational limitations, I might administer an academic achievement test in order to establish that they have the ability and capacity to understand the written consent forms prior to surgery. For those individuals who have the ability to comprehend the instruments, I generally administer the Minnesota Multiphasic Personality Inventory-2 (MMPI-2) and the Millon Behavioral Health Inventory (MBHI). Less frequently, I will administer a projective instrument, typically the Thematic Apperception Test. I generally rely upon the MMPI-2 and the MBHI because of the large body of literature validating them in various cultural and ethnic populations as well as with various physical ailments and disorders. These instruments are particularly useful in addressing many concerns for this treatment population. The MMPI-2 helps to establish whether there is previously unidentified significant psychopathology present, including personality disorder or somatoform disorders that could affect the outcome of the treatment. It is also of considerable value in further establishing risk of substance abuse or dependence, which may be a contraindication for the surgery. The MBHI provides empirically validated information regarding how the individual might respond to the post-surgery recovery. I also have at times administered additional screening tools for contraindications, including drug use or abuse, eating disorders, and similar concerns.

At times I use the Thematic Apperception Test as a means to further explore specific concerns in what is hoped to be a less threatening fashion. I sometimes need to explore the patient's interactions within the family dynamic for what they suggest about the individual's successful surgery and subsequent weight loss. Ordinarily I am able to explore this through direct inquiry and interview, but with some patients identified as less disclosing or that appear to be minimizing, the instrument is of some value in eliciting responses in a less threatening fashion. Often the instrument proves helpful in better establishing rapport. This contributes to the ease in exploring some of these family relationship issues.

Comments—Here the psychologist tells us that she is using empirically validated instruments with a fairly large research base, and a link between the referral questions and the instruments used is established. The instruments chosen seem to be reasonable for the task, and the psychologist is aware of their large research databases. Finally, why these test instruments might be of value in addressing questions relevant to the referral question is explained. Cultural and ethnic sensitivity are noted or implied.

The psychologist indicates infrequent use of the Thematic Apperception Test and seems to be aware of some of the psychometric weaknesses of the instrument, as she describes the use of the stimuli primarily for giving the patient a better opportunity to disclose in areas relevant to the referral question. (The instructions for this area ask for the candidate's theoretical orientation and how that theoretical orientation informs one's attitude toward diversity. This example does not address those things, which would more likely be done when this candidate describes his or her intervention work.)

More Problematic Assessment, Intervention, Teaching, Supervision Statement Example (with comments in italics)

In my multiethnic community I work with a large variety of patient populations. As a consequence it is important for me to rely upon psychological instruments that are highly versatile, particularly given that my diagnostic questions are primarily for my edification regarding their thinking and interactions. Most of my informal batteries, which are predominantly the types of assessments I might provide, include the administration of a mental status examination (the Folstein) and a projective instrument, generally the Thematic Apperception Test (TAT).

This battery provides me with the rapid screening assessment of neuropsychological function through the use of the Folstein Mini Mental Status Examination and a detailed assessment of the thinking and stylistic approaches that my patients have by using the TAT. Not only is this assessment relatively quick, which is a distinct advantage since I am not looking to provide detailed psychometric assessment, but my assessment battery is relatively economical. I am able to copy the Folstein Mini Mental Status Examination protocols and of course the TAT simply relies upon detailed note taking from the patient's responses to the projective stimuli.

Comments—The psychologist indicates that his goal is to quickly screen clients for interpersonal interactions and to rule out neuropsychological impairment, but it is unclear what this information is used for in relation to the services provided to these clients. It is unclear why there would be a suspicion of neuropsychological impairment but not a concern about the presence of psychopathology in the client population. The examining committee is left to infer how this combination of instruments is relevant to this individual's practice.

The psychologist has relied upon a projective instrument for assessment, when projective instruments are generally thought to be scientifically more weakly supported, psychometrically weaker, and are believed to be susceptible to cultural or ethnic variability. Additionally, it is noted that copies are made of the Folstein Mini Mental Status Examination, apparently without awareness that this is a copyrighted instrument and that making copies is a violation of the law (unless there is an arrangement to compensate the owner of the copyright) as well as a violation of ethics. Further, cursory review of the literature of mental status screening examinations would suggest that the Folstein, which is among the oldest formal screenings, is also psychometrically among the weakest. It has a high degree of homogeneity in its factor structure and does not broadly assess for neuropsychological impairment. Further, the established norms are quite limited and the literature suggesting the value of the instrument in diverse ethnic or cultural populations is sparse. Mental status examinations and intelligence instruments are known to be highly susceptible to invalidity due to cultural and ethnic variability, but the psychologist does not seem to identify this as a concern.

Topic 4: Discussion of Complex Professional Relations

You will need to provide one or more examples of complex professional interactions you have had involving consultation, supervision, scholarship, assessment, teaching, or intervention. These examples do not necessarily involve ethical issues and could center around resolving differences or identifying means of moving forward with a project or activity. Examples might include resolving authorship on a paper or presentation or identifying how to follow through on project assignments on some task in leadership within an organization. Other situations that might be used would include disciplining staff, satisfying demands from administration, or dealing with students on grading or final exams. You may want to try to choose examples that have a satisfactory or at least an acceptable outcome rather than examples that resulted in situations where no one was satisfied or, worse, when situations ended in litigation. While process is more important than outcome from the perspective of the examination, a poor outcome may suggest poor process.

While it is certainly permissible to submit examples when there was an unsatisfactory conclusion, there are almost certainly other examples with favorable outcomes that might better display negotiating skills and an ability to work around complex/conflicting situations. Since you will need to be factual and accurate you may wish to disguise as much as possible the identities of the other individuals involved, particularly if the example reflects unfavorably upon them. You would not need to use the person's name or perhaps exact job title but rather their relationship to you.

Better Discussion of Complex Professional Relations Statement Example (with comments in italics)

Much of my current work in psychology takes place in a local general medical hospital. It is not uncommon to be stopped in the hall by one of my physician colleagues to ask if I could see a patient about depression, noncompliance, anxiety, or some similar problem. These interactions ordinarily require 15 or 20 seconds and are much more of an issue of whether I have availability and infrequently an issue about the specific treatment issues involved. When I accept the referral, which I always do if I am going to be in town, the physician indicates that there will be a written order and I will be notified so that I will know who the individual(s) is/are and where they can be found. However, I have one colleague that is a very reliable referral source and more significantly has a population that is interesting and complex. I am always glad to receive referrals from that colleague. Unfortunately, that colleague, who also serves as chairperson for credentialing, most frequently does catch me in the public hall. Rather than asking if I am willing to see someone he goes into detail about the individual to a degree that they can be uniquely identified. While we generally enjoy a good collegial relationship he is also seen to be abrupt, thin skinned, and known to carry a grudge.

I have attempted on a couple of occasions to indicate, perhaps too subtly, that I was uncomfortable speaking in such detail about the physician's patient in a public venue. On a subsequent occasion I indicated that I was uncomfortable talking about patient details in the hall. I offered to speak to him on the phone about referrals but he dismissed the suggestion as an inconvenience. Initially I indicated that I did not have time to go into the patient details in the hall. These attempts were either too subtle or ineffectual. Finally I went to the physicians' lounge during a time that I know my colleague usually is present. I asked to speak to him and we moved to a small table in the corner of the physicians' lounge and over a cup of coffee I explained to my colleague that I was very uncomfortable with the amount of detail the physician tried to provide me in a public area. I acknowledged that physicians generally share more information and often in a more public area than psychologists do, and it may be more acceptable for physicians, but that as a psychologist I was uncomfortable with the exchange of information in such detail.

Ultimately I believe that my colleague was understanding of my situation and more willing to try to accommodate my concerns. Since I continue to receive referrals from this source and my re-credentialing has not been jeopardized I believe that we successfully navigated this concern. More significantly, I believe that I was able to sensitize my colleague to confidentiality issues, particularly in an era with national laws favoring increased levels of privacy (i.e., HIPAA, www.hhs.gov, and the American Medical Association Code of Medical Ethics, www.ama-assn. org, which similarly requires confidentiality of patient information).

Comments—Although this situation was uncomfortable and difficult for the psychologist, it is only moderately complex. ("Complexity" would typically include conflicting roles, needs, or demands, and may include a choice between imperfect alternatives, rather than a single problem behavior on the part of another professional.) The psychologist does appear to be aware that the physician is not bound by the psychologist's ethics code, although she does appear to be aware that at least with regard to confidentiality there is considerable consistency between the two professions' ethics codes. She does note that physicians are more comfortable in public sharing of patient data but her ethical concerns in this case stem from the amount of information disclosed in public and individual identifiability of the information, and not simply the different micro-cultures between psychology and medicine. The psychologist does not make clear whether her discomfort is due to possible harm to patients or due to a wish to avoid "breaking the rules."

This psychologist gradually increased the pressure on the colleague with whom she has a professional and financial relationship. Complicating these relationships are that the physician is identified as thin skinned and that he has significant influence on her service in the hospital since he has some control over her hospital privileges. Certainly it is reasonable to believe that with so many things riding on the conversation, the conversation will be difficult to have with the physician. In addition, most physicians act as if there were a power differential between psychologists and physicians, which makes the conversation problematic. The psychologist appears to have been sensitive enough to these issues to gradually begin addressing the problem and to ultimately address it in the physician's home territory, a venue that was convenient and that reduced the threat and likelihood of an unpleasant verbal interaction. Finally, the outcome appears to have been successful, although from the psychologist's perspective it is less than clear whether sufficient time has passed to determine whether there are long-standing consequences. Resolving the issue has reduced the psychologist's discomfort with the discussions and hopefully has served the physician by increasing his sensitivity to patient privacy concerns.

More Problematic Discussion of Complex Professional Relations Statement Example (with comments in italics)

I have a fairly insular independent practice. While I have many interactions with many people on a daily basis, I seldom have interactions with professional colleagues. Since I am not involved in academia I did not have issues with research and publications, and since I am not involved in a hospital-based practice I seldom have interactions with physicians, nurses, or other medical health care professionals. The majority of my professional interactions are limited to the occasional contact with colleagues when I need to make a referral or they wish to make a referral to me. As a consequence it has been a long time since I have had any type of complex interaction with a colleague.

The most difficult and complex professional relationship issue that I have had occurred almost 2 years ago. In that case I received a referral from a colleague. I did not know this professional well, but I knew him well enough that we made infrequent cross referrals when we had patients that we were unable to work with because of specialty, difficulties establishing a relationship, or the patient being much closer geographically or having time slots that better fit the patient's schedule. On the occasion of this referral this other psychologist referred a young male that was described as being depressed with substance abuse problems. I indicated that I was comfortable with the population. I had already obtained the release of information, and they provided me with more details. This sounded like an excellent fit for my practice. The reason the psychologist was referring at all was that the patient was much closer geographically to me than to him and the travel time was an issue for the patient's work.

On intake the patient did describe alcohol use and did describe depressive symptoms, mostly those of not feeling pleasure. He indicated that he was unemployed and that his family was helping with the co-pays. The patient revealed that they had extensive psychological testing from the most recent provider and that they had seen several providers in the past. After the initial intake we rescheduled, I requested information from previous providers after obtaining written consent, and I formulated the treatment plan consistent with the discussion with the patient. The treatment plan was fairly straightforward, involving cognitive behavioral interventions for the depression. When I saw the patient the next time I had still not received the requested psychological assessment results from the other psychologist. During this second contact with the patient he indicated that not only has he been seen by several other providers but he had some legal problems with some of the previous providers, specifically he had been accused of stalking the clerical staff. At the conclusion of the second contact, I immediately called this other psychologist, intending to ask for psychological test results and to inquire as to what he knew about these previous stalking allegations. The psychologist did not answer and never returned my calls. Ultimately, the patient became increasingly hostile during our contacts and was often seen waiting in the parking lot when staff would leave. I eventually terminated services with the patient by referring him to the Community Mental Health Center, which has better security and is presumed to be a better fit. I have never heard back from the other psychologist.

Comments—This unfortunate situation seems to have involved some manipulation on the part of the referring psychologist, but it did not involve a full interaction with the referring psychologist, was not really complex, does not appear to have had a good resolution, and does not appear to have been handled particularly well by the candidate. ("Complexity" would typically involve conflicting roles, needs, or demands, and might include a choice between imperfect alternatives, rather than a single, problem behavior on the part of another professional.) The candidate states that "his practice hardly ever involves complex relationships," but it is generally not a good idea to start out any work sample with a complaint that the question does not pertain to the candidate.

Ultimately it does not sound as though there was a good outcome either for the patient that was referred or in dealing with the professional that made the referral. Clearly there is every reason to believe that the referral source had more information at the time of the referral and was at best minimizing apparent threats or at worst withholding information in order to get rid of the patient. In either event the conduct appears to have been unprofessional, and potentially illegal. Depending upon state law and rule, failing to warn a potential victim about a potentially dangerous patient may be illegal. This error is compounded by unwillingness to provide patient records that are required to be released under law with the patient's consent. The candidate does not seem to be aware of the legal and ethical concerns and did not describe any consultation with other professionals or an ethics committee to seek guidance in the situation. The candidate apparently did not take any action with respect to the referring psychologist's actions. The candidate may well have some anger or other feelings about the conduct of the referring psychologist, but this is not mentioned or dealt with.

Topic 5: Examples of Specific Diversity-Related Issues

You will need to provide one or more examples in which cultural sensitivity and individual differences were evidenced in your treatment, evidenced in your interaction with colleagues, reflected in your research, evidenced in your assessment, or reflected in your consultation. Such examples may involve accommodations to religious holidays or attire and other culturally relevant issues. It is always helpful to review the APA guidelines on diversity in composing this part of the Professional Statement (American Psychological Association, 2002).

Better Discussion of Examples of Specific Diversity-Related Issues Example (with comments in italics)

My practice is in a medium-sized city and accordingly we attract a number of immigrants to the city. As a consequence we have many ethnic minorities, as most cities do, but we also have a significant immigrant population.

I was contacted by a local community charity. They asked me to begin seeing some of their refugees from Afghanistan, mostly for psychotherapy to address adjustment issues. After inquiring how much time was involved, I determined that my practice could not afford the time requirement, but I was willing to volunteer. They indicated that they had identified that a great many of their patients appeared to have mental retardation. They asked if I would be willing to assess the population and document their cognitive problems since this could eventually be useful for their receiving aid or even assistance with remaining in the country. I indicated a willingness to spend approximately 4 hours per week evaluating a member of their population and documenting my findings.

It turns out that most of these referrals were females. This was due to many males having died in the war, leaving more females to seek asylum. The females were unemployed and experiencing significant difficulties, even with shopping. These problems were not being identified in the smaller male population. The adjustment may represent cultural and educational deficits rather than innate cognitive limitations.

After reading several articles on the indigenous population of Afghanistan, it was quickly apparent that there were really multiple subgroups with separate cultures in the population. I identified from several sociological texts some of the characteristics of the subgroups. I did meet with members on the language translation team since many of the immigrants had poor command of English. Some of these translators had emigrated from Afghanistan to the United States before the most recent war and could talk about some of the tribal issues in the country predating the war. Others were native English speakers that were educated in the University both about language and culture. Finally, there were recent immigrants that had attended school in Afghanistan to learn English or had learned English from studying abroad.

Together with my review of the literature and in speaking to the collection of interpreters that had various backgrounds I felt that I had sufficient information that I at least knew how to begin the assessment work. I quickly established that it was improbable that I would be able to assess the population using traditional IQ tests because there were no English translations available for commonly used IQ assessment devices. Complicating this was that most of the females had a third-grade or less education. Since we know that education increases intellectual capacity, at least as measured by most available instruments, their very low educational attainment would run the risk of significantly underestimating their intellectual capacity. Ultimately I elected to rely upon assessments of activities of daily living in order to estimate their functional intellectual capacity. Even this solution of course is problematic since many of these individuals were culturally accustomed to a different lifestyle than they would have to attain in the United States, and may not have had time to attain that lifestyle. For example, most of the females for religious reasons were not allowed out of their households unless accompanied by males. Certainly this would alter their ability to respond positively to questions such as "goes to the store independently to buy groceries."

I explained, as best I could both to the agency responsible for the care of the immigrants in a general fashion and to the immigrants in a more specific fashion, what some of the difficulties were in making the assessment. In that regard there was awareness both by the immigrant and the agency about the limitations of the assessment. I documented these limitations within the record.

Comments—This psychologist appears to be faced with a very difficult task. Her knowledge as a psychologist alerts her to concerns about the use of standard intellectual assessment devices in other cultures, and a review of the literature did not identify instruments commonly used for psychological assessment that are available in translation for the population. Thus there would not appear to be adequate norms for any existing instruments, either home-grown or translated. The psychologist properly notes that education is correlated with IQ and limited educational participation adversely affects IQ scores. The psychologist would have been better served by providing a citation. The psychologist appropriately considered closely correlated analogs of intellectual assessment—specifically, adaptive scales of daily living. These too have problems in this population based on degree of acculturation, but because the psychologist is aware of the potential problems she is able to make adjustments to compensate as much as possible and to come up with an estimate that should be more valid than simply guesstimating based upon translated verbal interactions.

In addition to appropriate cultural and individual sensitivity, the candidate showed appropriate professionalism in providing volunteer time to use her abilities as a psychologist to help in the community. The candidate also provided appropriate feedback regarding general assessment concerns to the referring agency.

More Problematic Discussion of Examples of Specific Diversity-Related Issues Example (with comments in italics)

My practice is set in a large suburban area, and while there are a number of minorities in the area the population is large enough that there are many providers that are able to provide services to the ethnic minority community. However, I do have a contract with the local Community Mental Health Center where I see a number of individuals that evacuated from Louisiana after the hurricane. This population includes a lot of rural and backward individuals, many of them had outdoor plumbing and did not get to the city much before they lost their homes. This is a very different cultural population than I am accustomed to. However, the adaptation has been fairly easy.

For the most part these individuals speak with heavily accented English with some French words added. The language makes it a little difficult to comprehend but generally it is understandable language. Oddly, perhaps because of the stress, many of my patients present with what appears to be a high incidence of delusional disorder. They often believe that they have a hex on them or something like that. They attribute some of their mild somatic concerns such as headaches or stomachaches as evidence that they have a hex put on them. They report that they know that this is the case because they will find clumps of hair or small dolls with clumps of their hair on it. While their depressive symptoms seem to be better managed, the delusions remain and it consumes a significant amount of our therapy time.

Comments—The use of the words "backward" and "accented English" suggest a somewhat judgmental attitude on the part of the psychologist, who apparently is not aware that a substantial portion of the population in the Bayou Country of Louisiana believes in voodoo and other religions with similar belief systems. Many of these individuals believe in curses and hexes, and these do not necessarily represent delusions but are likely cultural phenomena. The diagnostic rules themselves would point away from such a diagnosis, since delusional disorders rarely present with accompanying hallucinations (if "seeing dolls with their hair on them" was hallucinatory), and delusions are not typically widespread in populations (although mass hysteria may have overlap with some of these complaints). Taken together there are multiple indicators that this was not a delusional disorder.

Topic 6: Ethics Example

You will need to provide a one- or two-paragraph long description of an ethical dilemma you have experienced. You need to provide sufficient detail that the committee can identify the ethical dilemma. In the remainder of the writing you should address how you conceptualized the ethical concerns and explain how you began to address the ethical concern and the outcome. You will find it helpful to review the APA ethical code. You should make reference to your understanding of the APA ethical code as it applied to the ethical dilemma and resolution. If diversity issues presented in the ethical dilemma you should also identify those and how they affected your approach to the other party and the outcome.

Better Discussion of Ethics Example (with comments in italics)

In my current employment setting I provide psychotherapy services at a state hospital. As it is a large state hospital I do not know most of the staff working in the six buildings on campus. In fact, having only worked here for about 6 months, I am surprised at how few people I know. From time to time the facility has to complete fitness for duty examinations on some of the employees. These are scheduled through occupational medicine and generally rely upon staff located at other facilities. I was recently asked to conduct the fitness for duty examination of an employee on campus due to the concern being mostly psychological rather than physiological. I did not know this employee, he was not a member of my department, and to the best of my knowledge I had never had any prior contact with the person.

I expressed concern to my supervisor, who made the request on the behalf of the superintendent of the facility. My specific concern was that there was a risk of an appearance of prejudice since I was a fellow employee. That is, while I did not know this individual, my employment by the same person at the same facility (i.e., the superintendent of the hospital) could result in the perception that I was not independent and impartial in my examination. I did not have any concerns regarding the examination per se since I have been conducting such examinations in the private sector for more than 15 years. Nevertheless, I did have concerns about the appearance of compromise of my objectivity in this particular circumstance. It was my initial thought that this relationship could represent a violation of standard three of the ethics code (www.apa.org/ethics/code/index.aspx), which describes Human Relations. Specifically, it appeared to me that there may be an ethical violation under 3.05 multiple relationships and under 3.06 conflict of interest.

In considering this request I initially spoke to my supervisor, who happens to be chair of the ethics committee for the hospital but is also a psychologist. I spoke to this person as an administrative supervisor, not as a colleague, since to do otherwise would represent another potential violation of 3.06, conflict of interest, for my supervisor. I thought it was important to explain my delay in scheduling the individual while I considered and consulted others about the potential ethical concerns. I was given assurance that not only is this practice common within the facility but that they had checked carefully to make sure that I had no knowledge of the person from any interactions I had within the hospital. Further, they felt an obligation to make sure that the individual would be assessed by someone that had worked in the specific practice area historically rather than someone with limited training. I indicated that I would talk about my concerns with colleagues in the community.

After again reviewing the ethics code and reviewing the Specialty Guidelines for Forensic Psychology (American Psychological Association, 2013) I did not see any clear violation present, although, again, I recognize that there could be the appearance of such a conflict and therefore a potential violation of the ethics code. Nevertheless, I spoke to several colleagues that are respected in the community and that worked in fitness for duty assessments. I also spoke with the state's psychological association ethics committee in order to evaluate whether they thought there might be a conflict.

The conclusions of my colleagues were unanimous. They did not see any actual conflict although they recognized that there might be a perception of conflict of interest. I documented my presentation to my colleagues and asked that they confirm that it was an accurate recollection and to forward me copies indicating that they had reviewed my summary and that it was accurate. At that point I then scheduled the individual for examination and proceeded with the assessment. The examination proceeded after obtaining oral and written informed consent for the examination consistent with forensic guidelines. Disclosure forms identified that we were both employed at the same hospital.

Comments—This psychologist appeared to be commendably sensitive to the possibility of dual roles and conflicts of interest. It also appears that she was sensitive to the difficulty that her supervisor might have had with regard to dual roles.

The psychologist correctly evaluates this as a forensic assessment and consulted forensic guidelines as part of her due diligence. She then consulted the state's psychological association ethics committee and colleagues working in the specific area of service in the community, and she took the precaution of documenting the content of those discussions and the conclusions. She seems to think that the appearance of conflict of interest is automatically an ethical violation (which it is not), and she does mention getting the evaluee's acknowledgment and acceptance of the situation as explained, which is an important aspect of informed consent in this situation.

More Problematic Discussion of Ethics Example
(with comments in italics)

Working in a large community mental health center with a small inpatient crisis stabilization unit I frequently have occasion to supervise practicum students. During one of our 6-month placements we had a student come in who received very high marks and very strong recommendations from his supervisor. Part of the student's rotation was seeing individual therapy patients and making initial contacts on behalf of the psychology department with inpatients. Initially, of course the level of supervision was fairly intense. First, the students would follow me and watch how I conducted these assessments and afterwards we would discuss it in supervision. Within a few weeks they graduate to where I could observe them performing these activities. Ordinarily that level of supervision requires another 2 months. However, approximately halfway into that two-month period one student appeared to deteriorate in his quality and level of attention paid during interactions with patients. After over a week of this observation I met with the student and described my concern. He indicated that there was nothing specific going on other than the stresses of graduate school. I indicated to him that he had to improve the quality of his work if he was going to complete the practicum with a favorable rating. The student acknowledged my warning.

During the following week the student did display greater attention to detail, was seemingly more alert, and was again living up to what was thought to be his potential. However, this improvement was short-lived. By the next week he was back to the behavior that resulted in my speaking to him in the first place. In addition, he was observed to have bloodshot eyes and some dishevelment. By the subsequent week the student's behavior did not improve and indeed he began smelling faintly of alcohol. I again met with him to confront the behavior and I asked about whether the odor of alcohol about him might be related to his deteriorated behavior. At that point the student broke down, acknowledging that he suspected that he was beginning to experience an alcohol problem. The student acknowledged drinking daily, although not on the job, but as soon as he left work he would have a drink. The student reported that on some nights he would drink himself to sleep, which accounted for difficulty in getting up and getting started in the morning and difficulty showing up in a timely fashion.

I indicated to the student that I believed that he needed to seek help and needed to report his problems to his supervisor at the University. The student indicated reticence to speak to his faculty supervisor about his drinking and went on to request that I provide therapy to him. I considered that this might represent a conflict under the APA ethical guidelines, specifically section 3.06 Conflicts of Interest. I believe that accepting the student as a patient and therefore receiving payment for services might conflict with my responsibility of supervising him. I reviewed the ethical guidelines in this area. The ethical guidelines indicate that there should be a reasonable belief that one of my roles could potentially conflict with another of my roles. Here it seems that the biggest risk was that the finances of being employed as a therapist might conflict with my role as being a supervisor. There is a long history in psychology graduate school programs, and indeed historically there was a requirement, that students enter into therapy with their faculty members as part of the training process. Accordingly, I did not think that this represented a potential conflict given this long history in psychology.

Ultimately I decided that the student would be well served by me providing treatment services for him in order to address the substance abuse problem. I do not believe that such services represent a violation of the APA ethical guidelines, specifically 3.06 because I do not believe that there can be a reasonable belief that being paid for services that are routinely provided to many other people presents a conflict. Certainly this bright, hard-working student would be best served by receiving treatment by a competent provider rather than risk his not seeking treatment at all and potentially continuing his substance abuse problem.

Comments—The psychologist in this instance does appear to have some knowledge of and sensitivity to ethical guidelines, although he demonstrates that he has not been keeping up with the literature either in supervision or the development of ethical standards. Supervision of students in training programs by faculty is no longer routine and is no longer considered good practice due to the dual relationship created with the students. By providing treatment for them and engaging in any other academic relationship with them including authoring papers, supervising theses, teaching them, class work, and so on, professors will very likely face a conflict of roles.

Additionally, the supervisor in this example has an obligation to the graduate school to let it know that its student is suffering impairment. Accepting the student into a therapy role now adds the additional complication of a conflict between the responsibilities of reporting to the institution that the student has a substance abuse problem and the therapeutic duty to keep confidential information about the client/supervisee. It is also very unlikely that the student could form an appropriate therapeutic alliance with a therapist who will have to decide whether the student passes the practicum. The psychologist/supervisor will face an impossible choice about the student's fate at the end of the practicum due to the multiple relationships that will inevitably inure to the student's detriment. The psychologist also has a duty to the patients in the hospital who may be harmed by having an impaired provider working in the hospital.

Topic 7: Ethical and Legal Status

The final portion of the Professional Statement is simply a statement that there has been no change in status with regard to legal, ethical, or board complaints against your license since you were admitted to candidacy. If there have been changes to your status then you should make note of them and provide sufficient detail so that the examining committee can decide as to whether or not the examination will proceed at this time.

REFERENCES

American Psychological Association. (2002). *Guidelines on multicultural education, training, research, practice, and organizational change for psychologists.* Washington, DC: Author. *American Psychologist*, 2003, *58*, 377–402.

American Psychological Association. (2013). *Specialty guidelines for forensic psychology.* Washington, DC: Author. *American Psychologist*, *68*, 7–19.

FOUR

Stage II: Recorded Practice Samples Focusing on Assessment and Intervention

GENERAL CONSIDERATIONS

In preparing the video-recorded Practice Samples the examinee is limited to 50 minutes of recording time for each of the two Practice Samples. Both recorded samples must be on one DVD or thumb drive, which must be playable both through Windows Media Player and Apple QuickTime. The Practice Samples may not be edited. This means that the examinee cannot remove or splice together pieces of the Practice Sample. However, since the Practice Sample is limited to 50 minutes and some Practice Samples may be longer than 50 minutes, the examinee may need to consider starting recording after 5, 10, 15, or more minutes in order to not exceed the time guidelines for the sample. Alternatively, you may wish to stop the recording at the 50-minute mark, even if it goes on beyond that. Certainly there will be some margin of error; perhaps plus or minus 10 minutes would be seen as reasonable, but submitting 180 minutes of recording would not be acceptable. Since the examiners could not know whether the first 10 consecutive minutes of recording had been erased or the recording had not started for 10 minutes, an edit from the beginning or at the end of the recording solely in order to meet the time constraints would not be considered prohibited edits. Prohibited edits are limited to edits within the body of the Practice Sample either to introduce additional information or to delete existing information to improve the quality or make corrections within the work. Any edits of the video should be described in your contextual statement that accompanies and explains the Practice Sample, so that the panel of examiners knows what they are seeing and understands why the video begins or ends when it does.

The examinee should remember that informed consent forms available in the examination (American Board of Clinical Psychology, 2011) manual need to be completed prior to the video recording. The video recording consent forms should not be included with each of the two Practice Samples. However, each of the two Practice Samples should contain in the contextual statements a representation by the examinee that informed written consent was obtained prior to recording. The candidate may also include the representation that informed written consent was obtained by including it in a statement in the video. The examinee should avoid using identifying information in any of the written documents or video recordings. Obviously since the video recordings are unedited it is likely that reference will be made to first names or places, but there should be an effort to avoid introducing the client by full name or some other uniquely identifying reference.

COMPLEXITY

Among the first questions that we are often asked by individuals considering Board Certification in Clinical Psychology or preparing for their video-recorded Practice Samples is about the complexity of the case. The question is something like, "Should I be trying to identify a complex, unusual, difficult case so that I can demonstrate the ability to handle such cases and my breadth and depth of knowledge?" Alternatively, they may ask, "Should I choose a case that is very simple so that I can properly prepare for all of the possible questions and the responses in depth?" The examination manual indicates that you should provide a typical case—this is helpful guidance. Anecdotally, after speaking to many of our colleagues that are Board Certified and some that serve as examiners, the consensus seems to be that you are better served by choosing your median case.

The thinking is that rare and unusual cases are hard to come by, and rarity itself suggests that it less likely that you would have a high level of skill in treating such cases unless of course you are specializing in the condition. If you are specializing in that type of case then it does not represent a rare case for you, the examinee. In addition, there is a risk that there will be much more controversy surrounding a truly rare case, and there may be conflicting opinions within the literature and among the examining committee. As a consequence, there may be much more information needed than the average clinician has at his ready disposal on such rare cases. Accordingly, the benefit of a rare case may ultimately be a passing grade on that portion of the exam, but the increased likelihood of a failed examination because of the complexity or controversy of the case could easily offset the advantage in establishing your potential success by offering a difficult case.

Alternatively, if you choose a simple case that presents no appreciable challenge and could have been easily completed by an individual with fewer skills and less training, it may be more difficult for you to establish that you have the knowledge and skill level commensurate with Board Certified practice. In this case, you may be well prepared in a simple non-challenging case and can answer any conceivable challenge or question, but the low level of skill demonstrated to work with such a case could serve as a disadvantage for you.

Generally, the recorded Practice Sample should be challenging enough to allow the clinician to demonstrate the breadth and depth of knowledge to deal with the clinical cases presented in his practice and that these cases require the advanced training that may be expected of a doctoral-level psychologist with 3 years clinical experience (or 2 years if 1 year is in a formal post-doctorate training experience). It is the examining committee's responsibility to identify sufficiently challenging questions from such a sample that the examinee can demonstrate his knowledge and skill level. In turn, the examinee should be willing to answer questions or provide descriptions of the service that are sufficiently detailed so that the examining committee has confidence in the examinee's knowledge and skill.

TECHNOLOGICAL CONCERNS

A natural concern might be how to go about videotaping the inter-action in your Practice Sample. Among the concerns is how to con-vince anyone to be video recorded in this very private and potentially embarrassing venue. Other concerns might be how this can possibly represent an adequate sample of behavior because of the artificial nature of the camera in the room. Finally, there are concerns about the mechanics of the procedure.

PRIVACY

We all faced the same concern with audio taping many years ago in our board exams. While video recording may seem far more intru-sive, we do not believe that this is actually the case. In some ways the physical intrusiveness of a small video camera is much less than the physical intrusiveness of microphones sitting in front of the client and the examiner/therapist in the old days when microphones were bulky and had poor acoustic abilities. More importantly, with people walk-ing around routinely carrying smart phones that potentially record everything we do or say, many people are much more comfortable with video recording now than they were with audio recording back when I (DBK) was audio taping my Practice Samples. In our training settings we get more resistance from our interns about audio or video recording them than we get from the patients. While anecdotal, we feel that recording is less of a problem than it once was, and it was never an insurmountable problem.

Again, relying upon anecdotes, we would note that the psycholo-gists, by having been audio and video recorded or watched through two-way mirrors in their training, tend to forget about video recording and the camera equipment fairly quickly in the session. The client fre-quently makes similar observations after the recording. Interestingly, some patients or clients will ask to review the recording afterward and may even find it therapeutic.

Perhaps better evidence of the feasibility of video recording the sessions is that the video recording standard has been present now for several years, and during that time people have completed Practice

Samples and submitted their videos. Ultimately we know enough about psychology to know that there will be many subjects that would like to be video recorded and there will be some that refuse. While this may limit the variety of cases you have access to as examples, it does not preclude obtaining appropriate case samples.

There has been some concern expressed by psychologists about recording with populations that require security clearances as part of their routine employment and interaction with their clients. If your Practice Samples would require examiners with security clearances we suggest that you contact ABCP to see if such examining committees can be provided.

REPRESENTATIVENESS

There is a large area of literature that is devoted to the effects of video recording, audio recording, and observations, either in the room or through two-way mirrors upon client behavior and therapist/examiner behavior. Most of the literature seems to concentrate on client behavior and is often cited as a reason to not video or audio record in forensic examinations. All of this literature is controversial in the sense that there does not seem to be a single clear answer, and this is one of the reasons that the question continues to spring up with each examination for the courts. There would seem to be little dispute that some interactions are changed by the presence of a camera or third-party observer. The magnitude and direction of the change remains in dispute. However, the examinee should bear in mind that if there is an artifact or a bias that is introduced by video recording then the bias is presumed present across examinees. Additionally, the examinee always has the option of recording more examples and choosing the one that best represents her work.

MECHANICS

Many concerns are raised about the technical/mechanical aspects of the recording. As noted in the instructions in the examination manual, the video must capture the faces of both the psychologist and the subject(s). It is also essential to do this in such a way that there is adequate sound volume and quality captured. This has given rise to the question of whether a professional videographer should be present to make the video recording.

The advantages to a professional videographer would be that one is more likely to provide high-quality video and audio recording equipment for the Practice Sample relative to the video recording device that the average psychologist might possess. In addition, the professional videographer could be expected to have more knowledge and skill with regard to microphone placement, camera placement, lighting, and settings issues than the psychologist in videotaping as an amateur. Note that the videographer's role might be limited to setting up the camera and audio with proper placement, and not actually turning on or off the camera, being present in the room during the Practice Sample generation, or knowing identity of the client.

There are clear disadvantages to a professional videographer. The videographer may want to be present in the room, which would probably increase the level of distraction in comparison to a camera alone. Certainly if the videographer were moving around a lot to get better shots of the psychologist and the subject this could be quite distracting and most probably unnecessary. There is going to be additional cost associated with having a professional videographer. A related concern to the cost of the videographer would be that if you were video recording yourself, relying on your own equipment, you could essentially make unlimited video recordings constrained only by time and the availability of willing clients. That number of video recordings with the professional videographer would probably become cost prohibitive if many sessions/examples were recorded. A professional videographer reviewing the Practice Samples, copying the Practice Samples, or present in the room while Practice Samples are made would need to be covered under HIPAA agreements and the standard consent form that ABPP provides would need to be supplemented with consent for a videographer to be present/involved. These additional documents (unsigned examples of them) would also need to be submitted with your Practice Sample. An additional concern about a videographer present during the video recording is that the examining committee would need to factor in potential influences or distractions resulting from the addition of another person to the recording area. This could result in greater difficulty for the candidate.

While we are confident that a professional videographer would improve the quality of the video and audio recording due to more professional equipment and expertise, this must be weighed against the cost. We would recommend the use of a professional videographer only if you have no video equipment and no knowledge or skills about even amateur video recording. We would also suggest consideration of the professional videographer provided one can be found that would set up the equipment but would not be present during the session.

REVIEWING YOUR RECORDED PRACTICE SAMPLE

Surprisingly some examinees do not review their Practice Samples. We do not know whether they are reluctant to see what they have done or whether they feel sufficiently confident in the quality of their work that they do not see need to review it. We urge you to review your Practice Samples.

Reviewing your Practice Samples should be an advantage to you by preventing surprises. If you make some type of error in your Practice Sample it is important to be aware of it so that you can discuss it during your exam. Clearly we all make minor errors and perhaps sometimes major errors in any activity in which we engage. There are many things we do or fail to do in our work because of our experience with the particular client that may appear to be an error or weakness in the absence of our individual history with that person. It is easier to respond to questions about these seeming weaknesses in our Practice Sample if we are aware of what the examiners are referring to when questioning us. Practice Samples are not expected to be perfect, but the examinee is expected to be aware of the errors made, and these will be more easily identified if the examinee takes the time to review what he as well as the client said or did.

In addition, reviewing your Practice Samples will allow you the opportunity to identify the time at which events take place in the recording. It is important for you to be able to identify significant events in the recording so that you may be able to discuss them or identify them in the description of your Practice Samples.

RECOMMENDATIONS/CONCERNS FOR
SPECIFIC RECORDED PRACTICE SAMPLE TYPES

Each of the two Practice Samples will have a 1,000- to 1,500-word description of the Practice Sample referred to as the "Contextual Statement." Part of the description of the Practice Sample will be contextual information. Depending upon font type, 12-point type generally results in around 250 words per page. Accordingly, you will have somewhere between four and six pages to work with in describing your Practice Samples. Be sure to include blank consent forms and release of information forms with each of the two Practice Samples if they are different from or additional to the forms required by ABPP. You will need to identify that you did complete the ABPP authorized forms but you do not need to reproduce them. Do not include signed or otherwise uniquely identifiable forms.

The required elements of the Contextual Statements that accompany the video-recorded Practice Samples are listed in the appendix of the examination manual. Please refer to the proper appendices when you are composing your Contextual Statements, since the requirements for each type are slightly different. The Contextual Statement gives you a chance to explain any anomalies in your sample, provide background information, and present information that the examiners may need to know in order to understand the sample while they view it. Detail and context in the Contextual Statement not only assist the examiners in understanding the Practice Samples but also afford you the opportunity to demonstrate your knowledge of the client and your understanding of the client's problems and situation beyond the brief issues addressed in the Practice Sample.

Practice Samples are expected to demonstrate competent interventions with sensitivity to cultural and ethical issues. In this regard your sensitivity to ethics and diversity issues, as demonstrated in your Professional Statement, should also be demonstrated in your Practice Samples. The examinee should be able to demonstrate cultural sensitivity and ethical practice in her Practice Samples and should be sensitive to those concerns in generating/providing the Practice Samples. In this way Practice Samples may serve as evidence of the examinee's adherence to her cultural and ethical sensitivity and awareness described in the Professional Statement. The examinee's Practice Samples need not be chosen to, nor do they necessarily, raise ethical or cultural sensitivity issues, but if present the examinee should be able to identify those concerns and how they are dealt with.

Some examinees review the recordings with their clients. This may prove to be a powerful technique to assist the client in the therapy. It may prove of value for the client in understanding why the examinee made a comment or asked a question. It may also prove to be valuable for the examinee by allowing for further clarification of what the client was thinking at the time of the response. While it is entirely up to the examinee whether to review the contents of the recordings with the client, it may prove helpful to the examinee during examination as well as to the client in his or her progress. However, we would not recommend showing the subject of a psychological assessment the recording of the psychological assessment administration since this borders on coaching.

Assessment Practice Sample

This may be limited to clinical interview, behavioral observations, or formal assessment with one or more psychological test instruments. As identified in the examination manual, if formal psychological test assessment is part of the Practice Sample, the recording of the procedure shall include rapport building, interviewing, or explaining the test results to the client and not simply the administration of the instrument. That is, the video recording should contain more than a demonstration that the examinee is technically proficient at administering some type of formal psychometric test instrument through careful adherence to the rules and procedures of that instrument's administration. It is presumed that the examinee has a sufficient level of technical competence to be administering the instrument; therefore much of the recording should address the ability to establish a relationship, to explain the reasons for the examination, or to convey the results of the examination. The recording should be sufficient to demonstrate that the examinee has the capacity to establish a relationship with the subject of the assessment and maintain the subject's interest in and cooperation with the test administration. Formal psychological assessment instruments may include cognitive/intellectual assessment devices, projective personality assessment instruments, standardized objective personality instruments, or any other standardized psychological assessment procedure.

This Practice Sample should rely upon instruments with which the examinee is familiar. This is not the opportunity to try out administration of an instrument with which the examinee is not familiar. The examinee should be sufficiently knowledgeable with the test instrument that not only is he technically competent in administering the instrument(s), but also that he has sufficient knowledge of the reliability and validity of the instrument as well as interpretation of the instrument that its use and selection can be explained for the subject in the Practice Sample.

The description of the Practice Sample in the Contextual Statement will contain information identifying the test instrument(s), if used, the reason for the examination/evaluation/interview, the choice of instruments or method, and the thinking behind the choice of instruments or method. Other important information might include how often you rely upon the instrument(s) or technique, as well as a discussion of the subject of the examination. Five-axis diagnosis with the current Diagnostic and Statistical Manual is required. Interpretation of the results of the instrument should also be provided. The formulation should be developed and reported as well, as any recommendations as a result of the findings.

Since an assessment Practice Sample may contain several hours of formal test administration as well as some period of interviewing, rapport building or discussion of the test results, the video recording may become quite long. It is important for the examinee to be sensitive to the 50-minute time limit for the examination sample. As previously noted, this may require that the examinee start the recording late, stop the recording early, or remove only the test administration portion of a continuous recording. The examinee should provide some type of indexing to the recorded material so that the examiners can more easily locate information contained in the Practice Sample that the examinee may wish to reference. Thus the examinee may wish to make reference to a time mark (i.e., 10 minutes into the recording, etc.) so that the examiners can more readily identify the procedures or skip ahead in the procedure on the recording.

Formal assessment reports are fairly common with psychological assessments, particularly when done for another service provider. If one is completed it should be provided as part of the Practice Sample. Specific identifying information in the assessment report submitted as part of the Practice Sample would need to be redacted before submission.

The examinee may wish to review Form D-2: Assessment Practice Sample to better understand the scoring criteria for the Assessment Practice Sample, available on the www.abpp.org website.

Intervention Practice Sample

This is usually some type of verbal psychotherapy, although it may include a predominantly behavioral intervention with little or no verbal interaction. Such predominantly behavioral interventions are presumed to take place either with individuals who are cognitively limited from a developmental disorder, as sequelae of an injury or a disorder resulting in cognitive impairment, or are very young children. Clearly, in these cases special efforts must be undertaken in order to establish that informed consent has taken place with the parent or guardian and been documented if age or infirmity precludes competent consent from the identified client.

From a purely logistical perspective, if the examinee works with verbal psychotherapy as a significant portion of her practice it is probably easier to provide a Practice Sample based upon an individual psychotherapy session with a single individual. Logistics and technical difficulties are presented by work with psychotherapy groups because of the number of individuals providing informed consent. Additionally, placement of cameras and microphones may be more problematic with large groups. Similar problems are presented for similar reasons with families, although couples are usually not as significant a problem with the exception of camera placement. With clients requiring purely behavioral interventions it may be difficult to obtain consents and often to provide mobility of recording of the interventions as the action moves around the therapy room.

The Practice Sample must contain a five-axis diagnosis relying upon the most current Diagnostic and Statistical manual. Details about the context of the treatment, the amount of time spent in treatment thus far, initial presentation, progress to date, goals of service, progress toward goals, and other significant information should be detailed in the Contextual Statement of the Practice Sample.

The intervention Practice Sample should provide information about the theoretical underpinnings of the intervention and empirical support for the intervention. There should be a discussion on the examinee's knowledge, skill, and experience with the techniques utilized. The examinee should also discuss interpersonal reactions with the subject during the intervention. The examinee may wish to review Form D-3: Intervention Practice Sample to better understand the scoring criteria for the Intervention Practice Sample.

Consultation Practice Sample

This is largely similar to the requirements for an intervention sample. The consultation Practice Sample is based upon a consultation in which the examinee was providing expert advice/information to (usually) another professional either in the same field or in a field that may rely upon psychological services. Thus the consultation may be to another psychologist about a specific technique, intervention, treatment impasse, or difficult ethical, legal, cultural, or risk management situation. Similar consultations might be provided to other professionals such as teachers, nurses, physician colleagues, or even consultation about management and personnel issues. A formal consultation report may be more common in this situation, and if one is produced it should be included in the Practice Sample. Again, it would be important to redact any identifying information in the report.

In the context of the consultation Practice Sample, descriptions of the individual being consulted, information about the reason for the consultation, and the parameters of the consultation should be provided in the Contextual Statement. This would include cultural and ethical issues as well as an understanding of the knowledge, skills, and limitations that the consultee may have. For example, if the person being consulted was a psychologist but predominantly analytic in nature and was attempting to use a behavioral approach, then it would be important to explain this to the examiners so that there would be a better understanding of the intervention taking place. The examinee may wish to review Form D-4: Consultation Sample to better understand the scoring criteria for the Consultation Practice Sample.

Supervision Practice Sample

This is similar to the consultation Practice Sample with regard to the content of the Practice Sample. The supervision Practice Sample differs in that it is an interaction between the examinee in the role of supervisor and a subordinate; either a student, lesser-trained professional, paraprofessional, less-senior colleague, or a colleague that is subordinate administratively. The supervision is clinical in nature and is not an administrative supervision. That is, the topic of the supervision example will be about the supervisee's interactions with a patient or client. While the supervision session may include purely administrative matters such as completion of paperwork, proper filing of reports, and similar administrative issues, the bulk of the interaction must be about a clinical interaction or interactions. A theoretical model must be addressed, interventional techniques must be explained, and feedback must be provided. Discussions of ethics or cultural competence may also be present in such interactions. Certainly if ethical or cultural issues are present they should be addressed.

The supervision Practice Sample is also similar to the consultation sample since the context of the supervision sample will be explained to the examining committee in the Contextual Statement. That would mean not simply a discussion of the context of the intervention that the supervisee was engaged in and the time and place of this intervention, but also something about the supervisee's experience, culture (if relevant), and similar topics. Similar to the consultant examples above, the Practice Sample should describe the knowledge and experience of the supervisee as well as the client that the supervisee is working with. The examinee may wish to review Form D-5: Supervision Practice Sample to better understand the scoring criteria for the Supervision Practice Sample.

THE SENIOR OPTION

For those individuals being examined under the Senior Option, video-recorded Practice Samples are not required, although the applicant may provide video samples if desired. The Practice Sample itself is broadly defined and must include at least one Practice Sample. The Practice Sample may consist of any of the activities previously described for traditional applicants, including: assessment, intervention, consultation, and supervision. In addition, the Senior Option provides far more latitude in the types of activities accepted, since most Senior Option applicants submit a portfolio of work products illustrating their contributions to the field (e.g., course curricula, scholarly presentations, books, publications, program manuals, etc.). These materials may include brochures, publications, video recordings, audio recordings, program manuals, and electronic slideshows (e.g., PowerPoint, flash presentations, etc.). The competency requirements for Senior Option candidates are the same as for all other applicants (i.e., adherence to ethics, sensitivity to cultural and diversity issues, knowledge of the scientific basis of Practice Samples, etc.), and each area will be scored, just as for a Traditional Option candidate. While awards, certificates, assessments by supervisors, and performance evaluations may be submitted as supplementary material, they are not considered Practice Samples under the Senior Option. The examinee may wish to review Form D-6: Senior Psychologist Practice Sample to better understand the scoring criteria for the Assessment Practice Sample.

SCORING THE PRACTICE SAMPLE

The standard for passing the Practice Sample (Stage II) is that the samples provided must represent competence expected of an individual with 3 years of psychological practice. For purposes of definition, the internship counts as 1 year of practice. Two years of practice are required beyond internship (although if 1 year of practice after internship is through an APA- or CPA-approved post-doctoral residency, that is considered 2 years of practice for the purposes of the assessment standard as well as application for ABPP). The examining committee will receive the individual's Practice Samples and review them in the specific areas identified in the Examination Manual. The current scoring domains are: Science Base and Application, Assessment Competence, Intervention Competence, Consultation Competence, Supervision/Teaching Competence (if applicable to the professional's practice), Interpersonal Interactions, Individual and Cultural Diversity, Ethical and Legal Foundations, and Professional Identification.

In Stage II, the three examiners will each complete the "Practice Sample" column of Form G independently of one another. The scored copies of Form G will be collected by/provided to the Examining Committee Chair. The Examining Committee Chair will review the three Forms to establish whether the examinee has been passed to the Oral Examination (i.e., Stage III) or has failed the Practice Sample Level (i.e., Stage II).

An examinee will be passed to the Oral Examination (i.e., Stage III) provided there is no more than one examiner that fails an examinee in a "Competency Area" as identified on the form. Each of the nine "Competency Areas" is composed of several subcomponents. The examinee is always responsible for eight competency areas: Science Basis and Application; Assessment Competence; Intervention Competence; Consultation Competence; Interpersonal Interaction; Individual and Cultural Diversity; Ethical and Legal Foundation, and Professional Identification. Only candidates with practice areas including Supervision/Teaching Competency are scored under this area of competency. As noted within each "Area" there are several specific subcomponents. To fail an examinee in a "Competency Area" the examiner must identify at least two subcomponents of that Competency Area as failed or identify one subcomponent as "seriously" failed.

If the examining committee determines that the examinee has passed the Practice Sample then that committee chair will notify the examinee. The examinee will then proceed to the oral examination stage and scheduling of the oral examination will be undertaken.

FAILURE AT THE PRACTICE SAMPLE LEVEL

In the event of a candidate's failure, (i.e., two or more of the three independent examiners on the committee each found two failed competency subcomponents or one subcomponent as seriously failed in any one area) the examinee will be notified. The notification will contain details regarding the reasons for the failure in order to assist the examinee. The examinee is encouraged to and may elect to submit new samples for another examination after paying the examination and review fee.

If the examinee elects to submit a new Practice Sample, he will need to provide the new Practice Sample to the American Board of Clinical Psychology National Examination Coordinator and the reexamination fee to the ABPP central office. A new committee will be appointed to examine the new Practice Samples.

The examinee also has the right to appeal a finding of "fail" by the committee. An appeal must be filed within 30 days of receipt of written notice of the failure. The examinee should refer to the ABCP Examination Manual for the most current information and details. However, the appeal must be based upon a procedural failure that occurred in Stage II or III of the Board Certification examination. Details of the specific allegation and failures of adherence to the procedures should be described in the letter of appeal because the appeals committee will only be evaluating the specific procedural failures and will not review the entire process or the Practice Samples. It should also be noted that the appellant burden is fairly high. The committee must identify clear and convincing evidence that the failure of procedure occurred and represented a substantial adverse impact upon the decision. The appeal process is limited to procedures only and the candidate should not confuse disagreements or perceived disagreements with the examining committee with regard to specifics contained in the examination and the examinee's opinion as appealable. For example, if the examinee indicated that Dream Regression Therapy was a viable modality for the treatment of tension headache and came to believe during the examination that the committee was in disagreement, the examinee cannot appeal based upon this perceived disagreement. Appeals are limited to procedural failures such as failing to examine the candidate's Practice Samples or having only one examiner on the committee.

If the appeals committee confirms a substantive procedural error identified by the appellant the primary remedy would be to allow the examinee to submit the same Practice Samples to a new committee for review. The appeals committee does not have the authority and will not be granted the authority to pass the appellant. Other remedies may be available and may be considered but, as noted, the most frequent remedy is to allow the submission of the same Practice Samples to a new committee for review.

REFERENCE

American Board of Clinical Psychology. (2011). *Examination manual for board certification in clinical psychology for the American board of professional psychology.* Retrieved from www.abpp.org/files/page-specific/3355%20Clinical/15_ABCP_Exam_Manual.pdf

FIVE

Stage III: The Oral Examination

*A*fter your Practice Samples are passed by your Committee of Examiners (Stage II), you are advanced to Stage III of the process, the oral examination. Your Stage II Committee will administer this exam, and they will already have your Practice Samples. The date and location of the exam may be determined in several different ways. The American Board of Clinical Psychology (ABCP) administers exams during its semiannual meetings (usually in April and October) at various major cities across the country, at the annual American Psychological Association (APA) Convention, and at the ABPP Summer Institute. These exams are held at a hotel chosen for the Board's meetings and exams. Alternatively, it may be possible for your ABCP Regional Exam Coordinator to arrange for your Committee to examine you in your own city (or nearby) at some other time of year. Any delay in holding the exam would be due to scheduling and Committee availability issues.

You can expect that the exam will be carried out with courtesy, collegiality, and professionalism. The examiners should view you as essentially a peer. You will find that most examiners understand a candidate's natural anxiety about the exam and act supportively and appropriately. The exam is a collegial opportunity with highly competent colleagues to seriously discuss and reflect on your professional life and how you function in its various aspects. From the point of view of the profession, the justification for Board Certification (in addition to helping the public to identify competent practitioners) is the opportunity for top members of the profession to attempt to define competence and to assist each other in seeking to be the best professionals they can be.

You will learn some things about yourself in this process. Most candidates, whether or not they pass, report that the entire process was a professional growth experience.

After a candidate passes Stages I and II, he or she is presumed to have the potential to pass Stage III. Note, however, that even though the Practice Samples have passed in Stage II, this does not prevent a candidate from failing Stage III because of aspects of the Practice Samples that come to light only during the oral exam, or because of the nature of the candidate's further explanations or elaborations in response to questions during the oral about the Practice Samples. It is therefore very important to review your Practice Samples before the oral exam and to think of questions that you can imagine the Committee might ask about them (further questions about the tests you selected, how you interpreted them, questions you asked or did not ask, reasons for interpretations you made, support for your understanding of the client, research support for your chosen method, etc.).

EXPECTED EXAM SCHEDULE

10 min	Committee convenes and organizes for exam
10 min	Candidate is greeted and exam schedule is explained
90 min	Examination on Curriculum Vitae, Professional Statement, and Practice Sample materials relevant to Science Base and Application, Assessment, Intervention, Consultation, Supervision/Teaching (if applicable)
10 min	Break
45 min	Exam on Interpersonal Interactions, Individual and Cultural Diversity, Ethical and Legal Foundations (including the ethical vignette in the candidate's Professional Statement, and one or two ethical vignettes provided by the Committee), and Professional Identification (including participation in the profession; current, significant issues facing the profession; use of consultation and supervision; and continuing professional education)
5 min	Exam wrap-up and final discussions
10–25 min	Committee members individually rate each competency domain and determine pass/fail

This is approximately 3 hr with the candidate. The Senior Exam follows the same schedule.

The basic schedule is to be adhered to reasonably closely. Significant deviations must be agreed to in writing, and if agreed to, will not be grounds by themselves for appeal.

The remainder of this chapter will present attitudes and behaviors that are relevant to your evaluation by the examiners, who are trying to determine your level of competence as a Clinical Psychologist. We are not telling you specifically how to "pass" the exam but are instead highlighting and summarizing essential competencies and competent behaviors of Clinical Psychologists. Hopefully you are already committed to being a competent psychologist and are trying to carry out these ideals and practices in your daily professional actions, so this will be something of a review opportunity for you. It is also an opportunity to imagine and practice how you would answer some questions that the Committee may very well ask, such as, *"Tell us what has convinced you to use and keep on using the theoretical orientation you have chosen,"* or, *"Tell us more about how you assess the effectiveness of your chosen methods,"* etc. Keep in mind, though, that you are not expected by the examiners to know everything or to do everything in an excellent manner. Use what follows as an opportunity to refresh your memory about some things, to recommit yourself to further learning and improvement in general, and to identify areas of improvement in which you wish to invest your energies right now.

HELPFUL ATTITUDES

Confidence

Organize your preparations in such a way that you can enter the exam feeling confident (or at least as confident as would be appropriate in that circumstance). Having a plan for preparing and then carrying out every step of that plan will help you to feel confident.

Humility and Openness to Differences

Being both confident and humble is appropriate in the exam, as in life. Don't try to be more than you are, or try to look like you are more than you are. Accept that much of what we do entails ambiguity and using one's judgment, so it would be natural for your solutions and your approach to be at least slightly different from those of the examiners. Only in cases where there is a clear professional consensus on an issue (for example, use of certain tests with persons of different cultural backgrounds, having sex with clients) or in instances of inconsistency (for example, not actually acting in accord with the theoretical orientation that you have described for yourself) are there actual errors. It's okay to have a different opinion from those of the examiners if you have good reasons for it. Be appropriately assertive in your answers, but don't try to debate differences or to "prove" that you are "right," for it's unlikely that you are any more right than they are.

Courtesy

Everyone likes to be treated with respect, including both candidates and examiners. Treating the examiners with courtesy shows them something about how you interact with clients and the public.

Reasonableness

As noted above, much in our profession is unclear as to exactly how it "should" be done. Be sensitive to and reasonably sure of your understanding about how "most psychologists" would do something (the consensus in the field) so that you are aware of the ways in which you have made different choices and so that you can then think of how you would explain those things to examiners. Treat questions and issues with reasonableness, and expect that same attitude from examiners.

Attentiveness

Pay attention to the verbal and nonverbal information you are receiving from examiners, particularly as to when they might want you to elaborate more on an answer. If you see signs of puzzled or negative reactions to your statements, ask the examiner if he or she wants more or whether you have answered the question that he or she intended to ask.

Appropriate Caution

On the other hand, in giving your answers, use caution similar to that which you would employ on the witness stand. Answer the question, but don't try to give more than an adequate answer or go on to provide information that you think is related but was not asked of you.

Collaborativeness in the Exam

Since the exam is to be collegial, it's appropriate to have a collaborative attitude, so that questions and answers have a mutually explorative component as well as an examination component. You are not automatically a friend to the examiners or their professional equal, but you are a respected colleague, and everyone can always learn more.

Self-Acceptance

Healthy self-acceptance is appropriate, and feeling good about what you do professionally is healthy. Self-acceptance, however, should be acceptance both of the positive things about yourself and the negative things. This means that you must know your strengths and your weaknesses, both professionally and, as they affect your work, personally as well. If you are not clear about these, you might ask colleagues or superiors, and ask them to be more candid with you than usual!

Self-Reflectivity

A very important but relatively new emphasis in training and in the conceptualization of competence for psychologists is self-reflectivity, which means being aware of your feelings and behavior, how your feelings are affecting your work, and how your work is affecting your clients (viz., the new APA benchmarks for competency). Instead of just doing what you were taught to do in graduate school, pay attention to whether what you are doing is actually the most effective way to operate. Notice your feelings in the course of your work (boredom, excitement, affection, distaste, superiority, etc.), and examine whether your feeling reactions to each client are affecting your work. Consider what these feelings indicate about how you are impacting each client. Step back and assess your strengths and weaknesses as a psychologist (and write them down as part of the process). Be open to sharing your honest assessment of yourself with the examiners, when it is called for by their questions. We all have areas of greater or lesser competence, and your awareness of the impact of who you are on your work (and making appropriate adjustments in response to this awareness) is more important (and more realistic) than expecting to show complete competence in every area. Don't forget that self-reflection includes noticing when your feeling state may be such that you should seek consultation or help for yourself, so that you can continue to treat clients well.

Openness to Improvement

Psychologists are expected throughout their careers to continually learn and to seek to improve their ability to help clients, not just up to the point of licensure or Board Certification. This involves "continuing education," becoming Board Certified, disciplining yourself to periodically evaluate yourself somewhat formally (including peer feedback?), and creating a program of change in response to your awareness of deficits. Share with the examiners how you have evaluated yourself and the plans you have made to improve, whether completed or not yet completed. (ABPP is planning to develop its own program for Board Certified psychologists of continuing education, structured self-reflection, and possible consultation about your strengths and weaknesses with another Board Certified psychologist in your specialty.)

Openness to Collaboration in Practice

Helping clients optimally nowadays involves working with other professionals (health care, welfare, social work, etc.) as needed, but many psychologists are reluctant to take on this extra activity and fearful of making confidentiality mistakes in the process. Since our society is complex (and getting more so), often working with persons of other helping professions (often sub-doctoral) can make a greater and faster difference in your clients' lives than your treatment does. Cultivate the humility and client focus that allows you to be comfortable with this other route to helping.

PREPARING FOR THE EXAM

The Examiners

The examiners will usually introduce themselves, telling you a little about their backgrounds. Their specific backgrounds should not make any difference to your passing or failing the exam, but pay attention in case their backgrounds offer you opportunity for some extra collegiality. At any rate, you will want to be sensitive to establishing and maintaining an appropriate rapport in the examination situation.

The examiners are trained to evaluate you according to your use of the principles of our profession and how well you understand and apply the principles of your chosen approaches to services, not on whether you see things their way. You should not expect that you will have examiners who practice in your area or with your approach, and you may need to explain your theories and procedures in more detail than you would if they were already completely familiar with your theory and approach.

Curriculum Vitae and Professional Statement

Based on your curriculum vitae (CV) and application, you have been approved to take the exam, but look over your CV and Professional Statement for any oddities or holes in your background that could arouse curiosity or concern in the Committee, because they will be perusing it in preparation for the exam. Decide how you would answer potential questions about your background. Be straightforward and unapologetic. Don't try to gloss over or obfuscate.

Preparing for the oral exam is an opportunity for a general review of your abilities, strengths, weaknesses, and personal issues and vulnerabilities. Take some time to reflect on your training and career. Think of all of the different aspects of your practice and also of other things you would like to be doing professionally. In what regard are you comfortably confident, and in what regard are you hesitant and unsure? Work on this for a week, and new awareness will come to you. Then, look at the overall picture, look for any patterns, and identify things that you would like to learn and areas in which you would like to improve. Be ready to talk with the Committee about your plans for professional growth.

You talked about your theoretical orientation in your Professional Statement, but the Committee will probably ask you about it again. Any coherent theoretical orientation can be acceptable, whether or not the Committee is even familiar with it, as long as you can explain it cogently and it makes sense as a whole. Practice describing your theoretical orientation (or the thought systems that guide your practice). If you are "eclectic," figure out how to explain your combination of ideas as a coherent whole. Anticipate questions that may be asked about theory and technique. Why did you choose your particular orientation? Be ready to explain why applying your theory and approach in your Practice Sample work is at least reasonable if not superior to other possible approaches.

Review recent research relevant to your chosen explanations of human behavior and problems and your chosen interventions. Think in advance about what further evidence would be desirable concerning your theoretical orientation. If some other orientation or approach has better research support, why do you stick with yours?

Be ready to tell the Committee about how you determine whether your services are effective. This is your chance to use your science background to improve the help that you give and to potentially contribute to the Psychological literature for others. If you are not collecting any such data at present, this is a chance to start doing so.

Review the items in your Professional Statement regarding ethics, diversity, and complex interpersonal interactions. Read them as if you were the Examining Committee, so that you can recognize ways in which you might have been unclear or incomplete in your descriptions and prepare to clarify those things, as well as to add afterthoughts that you have now about how you handled those situations.

Be prepared to discuss your motives for seeking Board Certification. These can certainly include benefits that you hope will accrue to your practice, but hopefully you can add some comments about the importance of competence in general and the importance for the public of a profession setting appropriate standards for the competence of its practitioners. The Committee may also be interested in your long-term plans in the field.

General Treatment Process

- Be prepared to describe your process of explaining confidentiality, payment procedures, ground rules, and so on, to clients at the beginning of services. If you use written client acknowledgments of these discussions, bring copies. Think of a few troublesome exceptions you have made or that clients have asked to make in your usual procedures and how you decided to respond.
- Be prepared to describe your clinical record-keeping system (and to justify any purposive omissions that you make in your notes based on your theoretical orientation).
- Be prepared to describe how you select goals for treatment and how you explain the treatment process to clients (e.g., informed consent), as described in APA ethics (American Psychological Association, 2010).
- Be prepared to explain how you choose the approach to use with a client. Be sure that you have incorporated the evidence-based practice philosophy in your practice decisions. (Read until you understand the difference between evidence-based and empirically supported.) Pay homage to the empirically supported treatments concept and explain why you don't use Empirically Supported Treatments for some clients, if you don't. Be prepared to distinguish your symptom-oriented treatment from any other treatment you do with clients that might have other goals.
- Accountability and efficacy have become important areas for psychologists. How do you measure or provide opportunity to review client progress or lack thereof? Be prepared to describe how you altered your approach with a client in response to lack of progress. If you do not use a written client measure of progress, be ready to talk about why not.
- Be prepared to cite examples of gathering valuable information from collateral parties (family members, etc.), when needed. Your work should not be isolated from the client's context.
- Be prepared to cite an example in which you sought consultation or supervision in order to better serve a client.
- Be prepared to describe how you coordinate the care of your clients with other providers (medical, social services, occupational therapy, vocational rehabilitation, etc.). Do you seek out additional services from which your clients could benefit?

The Recorded Practice Samples and Contextual Statements

Review your recorded Practice Samples and Contextual Statements in minute detail. Try to think of all the possible questions others might ask you about what you said or did, and prepare your responses. Here are some suggestions.

The Assessment Sample

With respect to the assessment sample, know why you made each interpretation of the data, and be ready to explain why you chose that interpretation rather than a major, reasonable alternative interpretation. Review what you know of the validity and reliability of each test used, and consider whether that information raises any questions about your use of the test and the interpretations that you made. Pay particular attention to cultural, contextual, gender, and age applicability. Looking back, would you choose other tests to use if you were to do the case over?

The examiners may point out interpretations that you made that seem not to be supported sufficiently by the test data, or instances in which elements of your summary conclusions are not clearly supported by the data or consistent with your interpretations. If they think that you did not answer the referral question clearly enough, they might ask you to go into more detail. Try to identify these things in advance, so that you can answer such questions.

Examiners may ask you about how your interpretations of a particular test relate to some specific recent research on that test, and it would be good if you are familiar with any major recent findings regarding that test. They may also ask you to rethink your choice of tests and your interpretations if the client had hypothetically been of another cultural background.

If the examiners note in the video emotional reactions on your part to the client, they may ask how those reactions might have affected your interpretations and conclusions. It is better to acknowledge (honestly) that you had those emotions and discuss them than to simply say that you are able to be objective despite your emotions.

The Intervention Sample

Be prepared to discuss your choice of treatment approach with the client (and why you did not choose other major approaches). They might ask what other treatment approach you might have chosen if you had viewed the client from a different theoretical orientation or if the client had been of another cultural background. They may ask about your recent reading regarding your treatment approach.

Know why you made each intervention and how it fit into your overall sense of what needed to be done. Think about how your interventions fit (or did not fit) with your theoretical orientation. The examiners might note how some of your statements about the client in your contextual statement do not seem consistent with what they see on the video. Are there any points in the session at which you would now prefer a different intervention or would take a different direction? If so, why? Examiners might ask what you think of another specific explanation for the client's problems or what you think of a specific intervention for the client that they describe for you. Examiners might ask you how your approach or interventions might differ if the client were of another cultural background. If there is an "empirically supported treatment" applicable to the case, and you are not using it, be prepared to explain why not. The examiners might ask you how you decide when to terminate clients in general.

In order to illustrate your efforts to keep up or hone your skills, be prepared to cite an example of where you modified your actions, either systematically or with a single client, in response to your theoretical or research reading. Similarly, think of an example where you changed your approach in response to the client's progress or lack of progress.

The Consultation Sample

If you submitted a consultation Practice Sample, review the sections above on assessment and intervention, since many of the issues raised there apply as well to consultation and to other client services, such as—

- Be clear about your overall conceptualization of the client and his/her problems/needs, and how your approach fits with your theoretical approach to consultation. Consider, theoretically, how things might have been done with this client by a consultant with a different theoretical orientation.

■ Know why you said each thing that you said in the video.

■ Be prepared for questions about your activities related to the client's age, gender, context, and cultural background.

■ Think about how your consultation actions would have been different if the client had been of another cultural background.

■ Be prepared to talk about your emotional reactions to the client and how they might have affected your behavior and your understanding of the client.

■ Check on whether all aspects of your contextual statement are consistent with what is observable in the video.

■ Think about whether you would now prefer some different interventions than those in the video.

■ Be prepared to illustrate an instance from your practice when you changed your approach to a consultation based on progress or lack of progress, or on your more recent professional education.

As in any client work, but particularly with consultation, clarity about which person or group of persons is the actual client is crucial. Examiners may explore with you what responsibilities you owe to the various people you interact with in the course of providing the consultation (some of them being clients and some of them not).

The Supervision Sample

If you submitted a supervision Practice Sample, review the sections above, since many of the issues raised there apply to supervision as well as to other client services, such as—

■ Be clear about your overall conceptualization of the supervisee and his/her problems/needs, and how your approach fits with your theoretical approach to supervision. Consider, theoretically, how things might have been done with this supervisee by a supervisor with a different theoretical orientation.

■ Know why you said each thing that you said in the video.

■ Be prepared for questions about your activities related to the client's age, gender, context, and cultural background.

■ Think about how your supervision actions would have been different if the client had been of another cultural background.

▓ Be prepared to talk about your emotional reactions to the supervisee and how they might have affected your behavior and your understanding of the supervisee.

▓ Check on whether all aspects of your contextual statement are consistent with what is observable in the video.

▓ Think about whether you would now prefer some different supervisory interventions than those in the video.

▓ Be prepared to illustrate an instance from your practice when you changed your approach to a supervision based on progress or lack of progress or on your more recent professional education.

In supervision, countertransference reactions on the part of supervisor and supervisee are frequently overlooked or discounted (even more than they are in psychotherapy). Self-reflective practice requires that you incorporate countertransference awareness into your supervision process. If you have not done this, a book on counter-transference-oriented or interpersonally-oriented supervision might be helpful. (This does not imply that you must accept a psychoanalytic understanding of countertransference, but simply that you are aware of and examine all of your reactions to supervisees and clients that are due to your own personal background or feelings.) Be prepared to describe methods that you use to evaluate professional growth (or lack thereof) in supervisees.

Teaching Activities

Even though a teaching Practice Sample cannot be submitted, questions could still come up in the oral about your teaching, especially if that has been a major part of your career. Your teaching would be evaluated based on the same kind of process-oriented questions that are used in assessing a candidate's performance in other areas above.

▓ Be clear about your overall conceptualization of teaching and how you would describe your "theory" of teaching. Be prepared to contrast your approach with other major approaches to teaching and to explore the benefits and disadvantages of teaching in some other manner.

▓ Be prepared for questions about your teaching related to your students' ages, genders, contexts, knowledge, and cultural backgrounds.

▓ Think about how your teaching approach might be different if the students were from other cultural backgrounds.

- Be prepared to talk about your emotional reactions to your students and how they might affect your behavior and your understanding of the students.
- Be prepared to illustrate an instance from your teaching when you changed your approach based on progress or lack of progress or on your more recent professional education.

In teaching, countertransference reactions on the part of teacher and student are frequently overlooked or discounted (even more than they are in psychotherapy). Self-reflective practice requires that you incorporate countertransference awareness into your teaching process. If you have not done this, a book on countertransference-oriented or interpersonally-oriented psychotherapy or supervision might be helpful. (This does not imply that you must accept a psychoanalytic understanding of countertransference, but simply that you are aware of and examine all of your reactions to students that are due to your own personal background or feelings.) Be prepared to describe methods that you use to evaluate the effectiveness of your teaching and the professional growth (or lack thereof) of your students.

Self-Reflective Practice

The essence of self-reflective practice is self-awareness—observing and knowing what you are doing (and following that up with wondering or knowing why you did it). As you observe and get to know yourself, you will have deeper and more firm self-knowledge that allows you to make sense of your behavior more quickly. This self-awareness will hopefully extend to all aspects of your practice—your office arrangements for clients and how you treat them out of sessions, how you get informed consent and plan treatment, how you deliver treatment, your awareness of how your behavior during sessions is affecting the client, your awareness of your personal feeling reactions to the client and what you do with that knowledge, and how you view and handle termination. Clearly, making good use of self-awareness involves empathy for those with whom you interact.

Self-reflection shows first in the Professional Statement where you have indicated why you are seeking Board Certification. The Committee may ask you this directly in the oral.

Your self-awareness will be explored in the oral, particularly in terms of questions about countertransference elements of your Practice Samples. Did your own divorce that was then in progress affect your interpretation of the test data from one or the other spouse or parent? Did your unresolved issues with your mother color your interpretation of the client's dependent behavior? Did your loneliness cause you to extend the client's treatment unnecessarily? The Committee may not know in advance about your personal circumstances or issues, but if they are oriented toward countertransference issues, they will note evidence of such issues (in the Practice Samples and in your exam behavior) and may ask you to comment on how your personal or professional issues might be affecting your behavior. Take a serious inventory of your personal and professional issues (write them down), and practice how you would describe or explain them if asked. Go through your Practice Samples with these issues in mind to try to remember your emotional state at the time and to identify any instances of your behavior that could be attributed to these issues. It's okay to have feelings, as long as you do what is needed to keep them from impairing your treatment of the client.

Exploring these personal and professional issues could be initiated by the Committee by asking you to list your notable professional strengths and weaknesses. They might then use their clinical observations of you in the exam so far to ask you whether some of those weaknesses relate to personality issues that you display.

Self-awareness comes into play, also, if you are asked to tell the Committee what kinds of clients you would not treat (and why). If you have not faced this issue, take time to consider if there are any personal or professional relative weaknesses that might indicate that you should avoid treating certain types of clients (e.g., suicide issues, borderline personality, adolescents, persons of other cultures, abusers, stalkers, etc.), and figure out how you would describe your reasons for referring these clients on. Be ready to describe an instance when you have referred a client instead of treating him or her yourself, due to these personal or professional weaknesses or vulnerabilities. Be prepared to describe how you handle your own feelings in reaction to clients who arouse difficult emotions in most of us—clients who have molested, murdered, abused, and so on.

Self-awareness is involved in decisions to seek consultation from other colleagues or even, at times, supervision for specific purposes (learning techniques in a new area or new approach, learning to deal with a type of client that is difficult for you). Be prepared to describe instances in your practice of seeking consultation or supervision and why you did so (including how you protected client confidentiality while doing so).

Maintaining self-awareness and a self-reflective practice takes focus and persisting attention to yourself and your behavior. Given our penchant as human beings for self-deception, we frequently fool ourselves about what we observe in ourselves, and gaining the observations of others can be very important to getting at the facts, especially when you are first trying to get a clear sense of your strengths, weaknesses, and countertransference vulnerabilities. It can be very useful (as well as interesting and rewarding) to join (or form) a peer consultation group that meets every so often to take turns presenting cases or professional behaviors of interest or concern. Be prepared to explain what you do to maintain self-awareness so as to give the best possible service to your clients.

One important use of your self-awareness is in your planning for lifelong professional growth and development. What measures have you taken or do you wish to take that will stimulate you, provide learning opportunities, and keep you on your toes in terms of self-awareness? The typical continuing education requirements for re-licensure have been found to be relatively un-impactful, so we all need to think more broadly about methods of professional development. Programs for recertification or "maintenance of competence" that are now being discussed and developed may include a broad array of activities (reading, personal assessment, peer assessment, attending presentations, teaching, personal therapy, etc.). Decide on such a program for yourself, so that you can tell the Committee about it if you are asked.

Exam on Ethics and Legal Foundations

Relevant questions regarding ethical and legal issues may arise at any time in the exam. The portion of the examination dedicated to legal and ethical issues, however, will include discussion of the ethical dilemma from the candidate's professional statement and of one or two standardized vignettes sent to the Committee by the ABCP (which will be treated by examiners and candidates as confidential and will be collected and sent back to the ABCP after the exam). The candidate will have ten minutes alone to think about the presented vignette. The candidate and Committee will then discuss the candidate's responses to the presented vignette and will discuss the ethical dilemma presented by the candidate in the Professional Statement. The Committee will confirm that no ethical or legal action has been taken with regard to the candidate since submission of the application.

An appropriate sense of how to handle situations with ethical and legal implications is key to passing the exam. You must be familiar with the latest version of the APA's "Ethical Principles of Psychologists and Code of Conduct." In addition to understanding (and espousing) the aspirational principles (do good, benefit society, be competent, etc.), you must know the specific prescriptive behaviors in the code (how to handle relations with clients, multiple relationships, advertising, setting and collecting fees, etc.). It is not enough to know the code for situations you deal with routinely in your particular practice; you must be at least somewhat familiar with ethical prescriptions for all situations. Study (or at least review) is usually necessary, and one of the recent books published by the APA on ethics and ethical dilemmas would be helpful to illustrate for you a systematized approach to analyzing ethical situations.

You must also be familiar with your state's ethical standards and requirements for licensed psychologists, and once again, it is important to know what you are supposed to do in major ethical-legal situations that you do not routinely encounter, including hospitalizing clients, having clients evaluated in their homes for hospitalization, supervising an assistant, research consents, explaining informed consent information to clients orally versus in writing, treating a child with consent of one parent only, and so on. Studying your state's policies and regulations for Psychological practice is essential to having a high-quality practice.

Knowing how to handle confidentiality is key to passing the examination, and confidentiality errors are a common cause for failing. *It is critical to know the APA ethical standards regarding confidentiality as well as your state's standards, if they are different.* (In your state, are you obliged legally to reveal confidential information to an attorney who has subpoenaed that information? Are you obliged to reveal confidential information if the court subpoenas that information? How can you protect your client's confidential information on the witness stand? Are you obliged to reveal to his or her parents *everything* your minor client says in session?) There's a lot to learn, and while most of us believe that we are practicing ethically, most of us are not at all sure how to handle the situations that we don't deal with frequently. Saying, "I would consult my attorney," is not an adequate substitute for having some idea of the ethical principles involved. A book on ethical dilemmas can help to bring these less familiar circumstances to your attention. Consider the recent books on ethics that have been published by the APA, on www.apa.org.

Be prepared to discuss how you guard client confidentiality in your practice setting. Do your clients sign in one after the other so that subsequent clients can see the names of those who previously signed in? Do you call out clients' names in the waiting room when you are ready to see them? Do you have other clients' charts on your desk while treating a client? Are all of your files locked up when you leave the office?

How do you view client confidentiality in the context of social media? Have you ever looked up or searched for a client on Facebook or other media? Have you been or would you be "friends" with a client via social media? Would being social media friends with a person cause you to later not take him or her as a client?

The Committee may ask you how HIPAA standards apply to your particular practice. (All parts of HIPAA do not apply to all practice types.) Be prepared to discuss how you implement HIPAA standards for electronic transmission of billing information (if you do this) and how you ensure security of stored and transmitted electronic information.

The Committee may ask you if you ever give your home phone number (or cell number) to any client and how this interacts with the importance for having professional boundaries. Be prepared to cite an example of how you dealt with a boundary issue (a client pushing the limits or a client seeking something from you that was not included in your original treatment contract).

Be prepared to discuss the fairly common (but illegal and unethical) practice of diagnosing a client in a manner that ensures that your services will be reimbursed by insurance, rather than solely on the basis of the client's information and symptoms. Be prepared to explain your "philosophy" of diagnosing, if it is at all different from the rules of the diagnostic system you are using.

Practice analyzing ethical situations. Prepare to assess, cite, and choose between alternatives, rather than simply "knowing the rules." It is ideal if you have a step-by-step system for analyzing ethical situations (that you can briefly describe for the Committee). Be prepared to cite instances in which you followed (or did not follow) reporting requirements for "reporting" in your state (child abuse, elder abuse, etc.). In many situations involving ethics, there is no one "right" answer, so the ability to cite and apply the various principles and guidelines to the situation and at least to clarify the issues as much as possible is important. Again, a book that analyzes ethical dilemmas can demonstrate for you a structured process for analysis.

Individual and Cultural Diversity

It is an ethical expectation of psychologists nowadays, as well as very important in providing good services to clients, that psychologists be as attuned as possible to multicultural and other diversity issues and that they prepare, in advance of having such a client, by learning about such issues and how to handle them. Be prepared to discuss diversity issues in your own practice. What is the diversity breakdown of your clientele (age, gender, ethnicity, culture, sexual orientation, disability, religion, etc.)? Are there clients that you do not assess or treat because of diversity issues (your emotions or lack of knowledge)? How culturally or diversity competent do you think you are? Do you have emotional reactions (countertransference reactions) to any diversity group that make it difficult for you to work with them? Be prepared to cite an assessment example and an intervention example illustrating how you took a client's diversity uniqueness into account in choosing and interpreting assessment instruments and in choosing and applying treatment techniques or approaches. As an exercise, think about a client that you have, and then think about how your approach or actions would be different if the client was from another cultural background.

Exam on Professional Identification

Board Certified psychologists are expected to participate in the essential activities of members of a profession, including participation in the profession's organization and governance, working to further the profession's development and goals, and contributions as a professional to society. These are the activities that justify society's acceptance of a professional group claiming to take care of an area of societal need.

As a professional, it is important to be aware of the issues and challenges faced by the profession. In recent years, diminution of income as a result of the struggles over health care costs, the intrusion of other professional groups into practice territory that psychologists previously thought of as their own, and difficulties of students finding internships are examples. An emerging issue is how psychologists will fit into the new health care environment that is being created by the Patient Protection and Affordable Care Act. Learn about these issues, and be prepared to outline them with your views on how you think they could be solved in the best interests of the public and of psychology. Reading (if you have not already) issues for the last year or two of the *American Psychologist* and *APA Monitor* will acquaint you with current issues, thinking, and concerns.

It is critical that the profession organize and structure itself, ensuring contributions to society by the profession and organizing the training and certification sequence for entrance into the profession. There is a trend in all professions in recent generations, unfortunately, to ignore the organization and governance of the profession, with the attitude that "someone else is doing that" or "someone else always takes care of that." Memberships in professional organizations of various disciplines (including psychology and medicine) are decreasing. There are many different options for participating in the profession, including local Psychological associations, state Psychological associations, APA committees, becoming an examiner for ABCP, being active in the American Academy of Clinical Psychology, mentoring, and writing for professional journals. Be prepared to tell the examiners how you have and will participate in the profession. Your voice and contributions are needed.

Becoming Board Certified is one way of contributing to the profession's development, as is promoting Board Certification to others. Be prepared to comment on how you plan to promote Board Certification and to engender Board Certification efforts to others.

It is part of being a professional, though not emphasized very much in graduate school, to "give back" to society. This is most often done by providing some services at no cost (pro bono work), but it can also take the form of participation on the board of a local social welfare organization or of one providing health care services for the poor. Be prepared to tell the Committee how you are living out this aspect of being a true professional.

Using consultation and supervision as needed in the course of one's practice and seeking continued education and growth are also aspects of one's identification with the profession. They are key responsibilities of being a professional. These aspects have been explained above under "Reflective Practice."

Emotions Regarding the Exam

Over the course of your education, you have had a great deal of experience in taking exams, but the licensing exam and the Board Certification oral seem to have such significance as global statements about our competence and worthiness to be psychologists that emotions in response to approaching and taking the exam need attention. Be assured that it is the intent of the ABPP that the Clinical oral be a collegial rather than an adversarial experience. Almost all examiners want you to pass (just as many of us starting out "wanted" our first Wechsler intelligence scales examinees to do well as we practiced giving the tests). Review "Helpful Attitudes" above and imagine yourself embodying these attitudes in the exam. Take an inventory of emotional reactions that may interfere with your exam performance. These might include embarrassment (for not knowing more or for not being perfect), guilt (for asserting that you could be good enough to deserve Board Certification), feelings of inferiority in response to older examiners, and responses to examiners of the opposite sex. Prepare yourself to deal with each issue that you identify (including how you might comment on them during the exam to illustrate your self-knowledge).

PRACTICING FOR THE EXAM

You have now reached the end of the long process of applying, providing data for ABPP and ABCP, reviewing what it means to be a competent professional, and assessing your status and strengths and weaknesses as a practitioner. In the few weeks before the oral, you may wish to actually practice some specific responses for the exam.

- Practice out loud all of your responses to the above "be prepared to..." questions, until you can say what you really want to say clearly and succinctly.
- You may wish to have a respected colleague ask you some questions in a mock-exam situation. (You may wish not to do this if it would heighten your anxiety rather than desensitize you.) Note your emotional reactions to his or her questions, particularly those that may interfere with your performance.
- Re-review completely all videos and written materials of the work samples *a few days before the exam*, so that you will be familiar with all details.

Responses to Avoid in the Oral Exam

While practicing responses to the above questions, take note of any of the types of responses below and explore with yourself (or trusted colleagues) why you might be engaging in them.

- Defending your failure to provide information that was required in the instructions for the Professional Statement or Practice Samples (there are no excuses for not following directions)
- Refusing to be specific about your orientation (on the basis that it is too abstract or complicated to be described, or too eclectic to be classifiable, or that you don't like to be pigeon-holed)
- Sticking with "eclectic" as your orientation, without specifying the different themes or theories that make up your brand of eclectic
- Speaking too quickly (stop and think before answering—it saves you having to change your answer; it's okay to take your time)
- Trying to answer when you don't know (making things up or giving a general hedging answer with no content—admit it when you don't know; you don't have to know everything)

- Striving to defend or not acknowledge a mistake (admit your mistake in a way that conveys that you can handle feelings of shame, that you can correct mistakes, and that you will be truthful and responsible with the examiners and with your clients)
- Responding to a consultation or ethical question by saying only that you would seek consultation yourself
- Treating just about any issue or question as being cut-and-dried (that there is only one right answer, or that clinical activities are straightforward or simple)
- Acting as if your theory can explain everything (since every theory makes assumptions and is context-dependent)
- Resisting giving your conclusion when to do so is professionally necessary, but you're not sure what to say
- Acting as if the rules that most mortals must follow don't apply to you in the same way
- Justifying what you did on the basis that it is what everyone else does (instead of explaining your rationale)
- Asserting that you don't have any countertransference issues
- Asserting that one interpretation is just as good as any other
- Asserting that you work equally well with all kinds of clients
- Asserting or implying stereotyped views of minority or special groups to cover the fact that you don't know much about them
- Putting too much emphasis on passing (approach it as a collegial, respectful opportunity to explore what it is to be a competent professional Psychologist)

During the exam, try to avoid the following:

- Apologizing too much for a mistake
- Putting yourself down for a mistake or for having a difference of opinion with a committee member
- Suggesting that on the basis of your status or position you should pass
- Trying to create a "buddy" atmosphere with the committee, implying that you are already in the club
- Putting down other practitioners or orientations, particularly by agreeing with a committee member's implied deprecation of them
- Siding with one examiner against another when there are differences between examiners

If you are seriously attempting to integrate all of the appropriate and ethical professional practices described in this chapter into your own work, you are doing the best that you can at being the best Psychologist you can, and you have nothing to be ashamed of in the exam. Be straightforward about yourself and your work. Readily comment on your relative weaknesses—not as something deplorable but as an aspect of reality that you recognize and utilize to ensure the best services for your clients (and that perhaps you are seeking to improve).

AFTER THE EXAM

At the time of the exam, the Committee will return your Practice Samples to you. It would be wise to preserve them until you are sure that you will not appeal the Committee's finding (which can be done only for procedural deviations and not for the judgment of the Committee about your passing or not passing). You should have no contact with the Committee after the exam. (If you should wish to initiate a non-exam-related professional contact with a Committee member, wait until after the total process is completed.) If you pass, the Committee will send a form certifying that to the Central Office, which will inform you of your results. If you do not pass, within 2 weeks the Committee will prepare a report of the exam citing strengths and weaknesses observed and identifying the specific criteria that resulted in the Committee's decision for you not to pass (and encouraging you to take the exam again).

The examination is confidential. Examiners do not use outside knowledge about the candidate that was gained about the candidate through the exam.

If you should wish to appeal, read the section on appeals in the Clinical Exam Manual and fill out the form for that purpose in the Manual. Remember, you cannot appeal just because you believe, from the exam itself or from the letter, that the Committee did not understand you accurately or did not make a fair and reasonable judgment regarding passing or failing from your behavior. You can only appeal on the basis of procedural deviations, and the only outcome of that is to arrange for another exam for you. The Committee's determination of pass or fail will not be altered due to an appeal.

If you do not pass, we urge you to strongly consider taking the exam again. Many people who do not pass the first time have passed the second time. You can use the Committee's description of your weaknesses to shore up your knowledge in certain areas before you retake the exam. (Taking the examination again entails submitting new Practice Samples and again passing Stage II.)

You may provide written feedback to ABCP about the examination (Form M) and your experience of it.

REFERENCE

American Psychological Association. (2010). *Ethical principles of psychologists and code of conduct*. Washington, DC: American Psychological Association. Retrieved from www.apa.org/ethics/code/index.aspx

SIX

Life After Examination

Congratulations! If you worked at breakneck speed you spent probably 9 months applying for the examination, being examined, and now finally you have received notification of your success. More typically you have spent approximately 18 months until you received your letter of congratulations upon having been awarded your ABPP diploma in Clinical Psychology. Having achieved this hard-earned distinction you now have freed up some time in your life that had been spent preparing work samples and preparing for oral examinations. You are probably wondering how you are going to spend all the extra time you have freed up. First you will probably start on all the things you put off doing while preparing for your board examination. Next, however, you have many options available to you after completing your Board Certification. You can become involved with ABPP and with the Academy, you can begin mentoring, you may begin to pursue other leadership roles within your profession, and you can remain serious about continuing professional development. Don't forget to contact ABPP Central Office (office@ABPP.org) for your 10 American Psychological Association (APA)-Approved CE credits for earning your Board Certification.

YOUR PRACTICE

As noted in Chapter 1, as a Board Certified Clinical Psychologist, you will have some enhanced practice opportunities. Many provider panels prefer Board Certified psychologists, so you may wish to expand your panel affiliations. You are now in a better position to be regarded in court as an expert witness who is truly expert, so you may wish to engage in or expand your forensic activities. If you work in a hospital, being Board Certified may make you eligible to be a part of the Medical Staff, or it may make you eligible (or more desirable) for positions in the growing number of integrated care facilities.

For those who are employed, a few employers offer higher pay or bonuses to those who are Board Certified. Currently the Department of Defense, Public Health Service, and Veterans Administration offer such opportunities. If your employer does not, then you can begin to advocate for a pay differential or bonus where you work!

Since some potential clients recognize the value of Board Certification in physicians (and now in psychologists) you may wish to make your Board Certification known. You can proudly put your Board Certification certificate on your wall! The Academy website has a layout for a brief pamphlet on Board Certification that you can print yourself and leave in your waiting room for clients to see and to take to others. Be sure that the ABPP and AACP website directories have you listed and listed correctly. You can engage in public service talks to groups likely to need services and can include education about Board Certification in your presentation.

You may wish to consider expanding your practice locations, since currently 36 of the 50 states make it easier for those who are Board Certified to gain licensure through reciprocity.

Finally, you can cultivate relationships with other Board Certified psychologists in your area, since they form a useful pool of knowledgeable and competent peers with whom to consult or refer.

AMERICAN ACADEMY OF CLINICAL PSYCHOLOGY

One of the first things you might want to consider doing is becoming a member of the American Academy of Clinical Psychology (AACP). For a relatively modest fee (currently $50) you may become a member of the Academy. Voting membership is presently only open to those who have been awarded their certification diploma. You should receive an invitation letter from the AACP shortly after receiving notification of the award of your diploma. Of course you may already be involved with the AACP either because you sought mentorship previously or perhaps because you have been in one of the affiliated nonvoting membership classes that are being considered for establishment by the AACP.

As a voting member of the AACP you may enjoy a number of benefits. You and your practice information will be listed in the AACP website's directory, which may be viewed by the public. There is a dedicated listserv available to members, which addresses things that affect certification, certificate holders, and issues that might be of interest to Board Certified psychologists. The Academy also offers discounts on malpractice insurance. Board Certified psychologists that are members of the AACP have the opportunity to become Fellows of the AACP. (The Academy is presently reviewing requirements and standards for Fellowship.) In addition there is a journal of the Academy, which contains information about Clinical Psychology and the practice of Clinical Psychology as well as other professional issues that may be of interest to Board Certified psychologists. The Academy also offers to its members opportunity for continuing education.

MENTORING

Board Certified psychologists may contribute to the field by mentoring psychologists at all stages in the process of seeking Board Certification. While some types of mentoring were available to you prior to becoming a Board Certified psychologist, you now have the additional opportunity to serve in a formal role as a mentor for other individuals considering or seeking Board Certification. In this role you may assist individuals in understanding the value of Board Certified psychologist status as well as educating them with regard to the procedures and your experiences in seeking to become a Board Certified psychologist.

The AACP provides guidelines for mentors and assists interested psychologists in finding mentors. The AACP can consult with you regarding mentorship, and assist you in finding individuals seeking mentors. In addition, the AACP may provide additional support in the form of clarification of the certification processes, which may have changed since you were awarded your diploma, such as technical issues that did not affect you or were not relevant to your examination. For example, if you are serving as a mentor to a senior psychologist while you received your diploma under the traditional certification rules or, conversely, if you received your diploma under the Senior provisions and you are mentoring someone seeking Board Certification under the traditional certification rules you may need some assistance or guidance on areas in which you have less familiarity.

Division 42 of the APA (Psychologists in Independent Practice) has a program to connect its Board Certified members who are seeking Senior Psychologist certification with the Division's own internal mentors. If you are a member of Division 42, mentoring through Division 42 will allow you to assist colleagues seeking Board Certification while contributing to Division 42 and to ABPP.

BECOMING AN EXAMINER

As a Board Certified psychologist you may wish to consider volunteering to become an examiner. This can be a very rewarding contribution to the field, although it is time consuming. Since there are over 1200 currently Board Certified Clinical Psychologists, there are enough potential examiners in this pool to ensure that examining is not a burden to any who volunteer to examine. Examining Committee chairs often serve several committees at one time because of their experience, but committee members generally do not have as many opportunities to serve as do the chairs. Serving on examining committees is limited by your time availability, location, and the amount of time required. These factors are considered by the examination committee chair and may make serving or being called upon to serve on the committees less (or more) likely.

If you apply and are chosen as an examiner, you will be responsible for reviewing the candidate's Professional Statements and Practice Samples. If the candidate succeeds in moving on to Stage III (the Oral Examination) you would be an examiner on the oral examining committee. Should you choose to continue on with examining committees, you may seek to become a committee chair. Examiners probably vary in preparation time (reading the Curriculum Vitae and Professional Statement and reviewing the two videos while taking notes of questions to ask), but this can take 4 to 7 hours depending on the materials. Following this preparation, you would have the half-day exam time, plus any travel involved. Ordinarily the examiner will want to take time after reviewing the Practice Sample to consider the kinds of questions he or she might want the candidate to answer. While the questions from the oral examiner generally follow from the candidate's statements within the exam, there are also questions that follow naturally from reviewing the Practice Sample, and it is handy to have those available at the time of the examination.

An additional benefit of serving as an examiner is the opportunity to brush up on an area or perhaps expose yourself to an area of psychology or population within psychology that you do not ordinarily deal with. This will broaden your knowledge and skill while serving the psychology community.

PROMOTING BOARD CERTIFICATION

Those who are Board Certified are expected to promote Board Certification, so that more and more psychologists affirm the importance and value of Board Certification by becoming Board Certified themselves. You can speak to your colleagues about the importance of Board Certification and urge them to apply. You may serve as a mentor. You can involve yourself in the affairs of ABPP and AACP, perhaps serving on committees or boards. Look at the ABPP journal, *The Specialist*, to see how the ABPP is organized and managed, and read the AACP minutes on the AACP website to see what you might be interested in doing for the Academy. You can write about Board Certification for local or national publications (including the newsletter of your local psychological association and the newsletter of your own organization or psychology staff). You can give brief presentations to graduate students (and faculty) at nearby graduate schools. Please be an advocate for ABPP and for Board Certification!

CONTINUING PROFESSIONAL DEVELOPMENT

Simply as responsible professionals but also as representatives of Board Certification, those who are Board Certified have a special obligation to maintain competence, keep up to date on professional practices, and continue to develop as professionals throughout their careers. Current re-licensure requirements for courses are not adequate for this, and we are all familiar with the "square-filling" aspect of "getting enough credits," sometimes at the last minute! ABPP is developing a Maintenance of Certification program for Board Certified psychologists, which is expected to have a 10-year cycle, with submission of a single year's professional development activities (including teaching, taking courses, volunteering in professional organizations, supervising, consulting, outcomes research, etc.) and a review of the psychologist's professional development activities as well as his or her personal plan for ongoing learning and development. Use what you have learned about your strengths and weaknesses during the Board Certification process to set down on paper your own professional development program, now, with what you want to learn and how you will go about it.

Due to the isolation of many professional psychologists, joining with other psychologists for regular case and issue consultation is particularly useful for maintaining competence. If you are not already involved in a regular consultation with someone, think of colleagues that you know with whom you would like to consult, and form a group!

Be proud of your achievement of ABPP Board Certification! You have demonstrated your competence and earned a place among Board Certified psychologists. Let others know. (Many newspapers will print a brief announcement for free.)

PROVIDING FORENSIC SERVICES

Many Clinical Psychologists provide some forensic services as part of their usual services. Board Certification in Clinical Psychology is often helpful in expanding these services. Generally attorneys, particularly when seeking experts for trial by jury, will try to find psychologists that are Board Certified. The reasoning has varied origins. Since many psychiatrists practice forensic work as well and virtually all psychiatrists are Board Certified, the attorney may feel that it is important for the judge and jury to know that their expert is also Board Certified. This is seen as a means of leveling the playing ground so that similarly credentialed experts, even if representing different fields, will be testifying.

There are several other reasons that an attorney may wish to have or prefer to have a Board Certified psychologist over a psychologist who is not. Board Certification is often perceived by the public as a desirable credential even if it is not known precisely what the credential represents. Since attorneys themselves may seek Board Certification in their specialties, they have some general understanding about the meaning of Board Certification as a credential and this may serve to cause them to seek providers that are Board Certified. As a result, if the attorney is not looking for an academic psychologist but for a practicing psychologist, she is more likely to choose one that is Board Certified if given the opportunity.

Board Certification in Clinical Psychology does not make you an expert in forensic psychology. To practice in forensic psychology you must be knowledgeable about and conversant with the issues of working in the court system and forensic psychology in general. This will enhance your credibility as well as your success as an expert. Forensic psychology practitioners should be aware of and sensitive to the forensic psychology guidelines and ethics, which are more extensive than and slightly different from those that guide psychological services in general. The psychologist does not just start to work in forensic psychology. He must learn about forensic psychology, seek training in forensic psychology, and seek supervision or consultation for forensic services.

GETTING A PAY RAISE

Board Certified psychologists in the Federal system are eligible for a one-step pay raise for Board Certification. The rules actually indicate that this is up to the institution or facility although in practice it is our understanding that the step advance is universally accepted throughout the Department of Defense and Federal employment served by civil service. Unfortunately for those psychologists that are already advanced in their field and are at the top of their pay grade there is no opportunity for a one-step increase. Some institutions and facilities have tried to reinforce the attainment of Board Certification for those employees that are at their maximum step by providing the maximum performance pay bonus eligible for that year, although, of course, there have been some years when the federal government did not authorize performance pay bonuses.

Psychologists employed by state government tell me (DBK) that sometimes their employer recognizes their attaining Board Certification and provide some kind of financial award. We would certainly encourage you, if you are in a state agency, to pursue this, although state budgets tend to be more volatile than federal budgets and we are not aware of any state with a formal policy to provide pay raises for psychologists that become Board Certified.

Psychologists working in the private sector occasionally get financial awards or pay raises based on having attained Board Certification. This is up to the employer and/or institution employing the psychologist. We would encourage you to have a discussion with your employer once you have obtained Board Certification.

The majority of psychologists are currently employed as independent practitioners. For those psychologists that are working in primarily cash-based practices, one may well be able to increase fees and receive increased fees based upon having become Board Certified. However, most insurance companies and third-party reimbursement programs do not recognize Board Certification with regard to reimbursement rates. You may try to negotiate with the insurance company or third-party payer for a better rate based upon having been recognized by your peers for the quality of your work, but ultimately your fees are going to be dependent upon the generosity of the company, the availability of other providers, and the company's perception of quality services as part of the network.

LEADERSHIP

Leadership is an important quality that is sought in Board Certified Psychologists and as a consequence many are in or were in leadership. It is commonly known that Board Certification is an advantage in seeking office within psychology. To the extent that Board Certification reflects an interest in leadership and that it reflects that you are a well-qualified psychologist, it is reasonable to believe that such individuals would be good candidates for leadership within the field. If you are currently in leadership then perhaps your diploma will not appreciably change others' perception of you as a leader. However, if you are not in leadership or have not been in leadership, a diploma will, in the eyes of many, serve as an indication of characteristics that are seen in leaders. We would encourage you to consider a more active role in leadership in the profession since good leaders are always needed in any field of endeavor.

We hope that this book was helpful to you in your journey toward Board Certification.

Appendix A: Mentoring Policies and Procedures of the American Academy of Clinical Psychology

INTRODUCTION

The Academy provides mentors upon request to the American Board of Professional Psychology (ABPP) Board Certification candidates as well as those interested in applying for Certification. The fact that mentoring is available does not suggest that all applicants "need" or should engage in a mentoring relationship in order to obtain the Clinical ABPP. Nevertheless, mentoring is available to anyone interested in obtaining Clinical Certification, and may be particularly useful for those with special concerns, questions, or undue anxieties.

GOALS

Mentorship has several goals:

1. To provide information to potential candidates that will help them begin the certification process.
2. To provide information that will guide candidates through the ABPP certification process.
3. To help alleviate unnecessary anxiety and concern about the certification process, especially the oral examination.
4. To help the candidate ensure that educational background, Professional Statement, and Practice are consistent with each other, or that unusual variations are accounted for.

MENTORS

1. Mentors must be ABPP Board Certified in Clinical Psychology.
2. There is no fee for providing mentoring assistance.
3. Before providing mentoring assistance, the mentor must read the Clinical Examination Manual, which describes the Professional Statement, Practice Samples, and exam criteria/scoring. Special attention should be given to Sections V (Practice Samples), VI (Oral Examination), and VII (Scoring Criteria).

PROCEDURES

Mentees

1. Requests for mentors should be directed to the current Mentoring Coordinator, the current Academy President, or from the Academy Office Administrator. Contact information can be found on the Academy website at www.aacpsy.org.
2. Mentees may request a mentor at any stage of the ABPP process, including before an application has been filed or after a failed oral examination.
3. Once provided with a mentor, mentees will be referred to the **Academy's Mentoring Policies and Procedures** (found at the Academy's website www.aacpsy.org) as well as the **Clinical Examination Manual** (found at the Academy's website under "Board Certification" or directly from the ABPP website at www.abpp.org).
4. Mentees will be asked to complete Evaluation Forms yearly and at the completion of the ABPP process.

Mentors

1. Mentors are assigned without regard to geographic location, theoretical orientation, or work setting since mentoring is generic and the **Clinical Examination Manual** applies to all applicants.
2. Once a mentor is assigned a mentee, the mentor should contact the mentee immediately, expressing eagerness to assist, encouraging

the mentee to complete the certification process expeditiously, and inviting the mentee to contact him/her with questions or concerns.

3. Mentoring contacts may be made by any appropriate means, including e-mail, telephone, or face-to-face if time and location permit.

4. Mentors are cautioned against allowing the relationship to become more personal than professional, since this can lead to confusion about loyalties and commitments.

5. Interactions with mentees will be collegial. There is no set limit to contacts, except for the mentor's time availability and preference.

6. Mentors should be very careful to provide accurate information to mentees, as this can make the difference between passing and failing. If there is any uncertainty, it is advisable for the Mentor to check the Manual before providing information. Since the examination Manual, including exam philosophy and procedures, may be updated several times a year, mentors will review the current examination Manual at least twice yearly in order to ensure that the provided information is current and accurate. If uncertainty remains, mentors should check with the American Board of Clinical Psychology (ABCP) Examination Materials Reviewer or with the appropriate Regional Exam Coordinator.

7. Mentors provide assistance that will enable the candidate to prepare adequately for the Clinical ABPP process and to provide an appropriate Professional Statement and Practice Samples. "Appropriate" in this context means fulfilling the content requirements and providing a clear and useful picture of the candidate and the candidate's professional work.

8. Mentors will not review Practice Samples, but may discuss them with the mentee. Mentors may advise that a proposed Practice Sample would clearly not be acceptable to the examiners. (See examples below.)

9. Guidance to those mentored may include explanations tailored to the needs of each applicant concerning the philosophy, structure, and rationale for the Board Certification processes, as well as general descriptions of the expectations of examiners for candidate clinical competence. It is the hope that such mentoring will help mentees better prepare their Professional Statements, Practice Samples, know how to describe their practice orientation, and be

prepared to answer questions about their work as well as ethical issues they may encounter during the oral examination.

10. Mentors may raise questions about possible deficits in the mentee's knowledge and skills, and may advise the mentee that a proposed sample would clearly not be acceptable to the examiners. Mentors may, on occasion, recommend independent readings, courses, and supervision that might be helpful in the mentee's development of further skills.

11. Examples of helpful and appropriate mentoring include, but are not limited to:

    a. Pointing out that the ethical dilemma in the Professional Statement is not really a dilemma but merely an interpersonal conflict.

    b. Advising that a proposed Practice Sample would not adequately demonstrate skills commensurate with a specialist in clinical psychology. For example, educating Masters-level therapists in a community mental health setting about the symptoms and treatment of a clinical disorder.

    c. Indicating that the proposed treatment Practice Sample would be inconsistent with the mentee's educational and supervisory background. For example, a mentee's educational background in CBT presenting a case utilizing psychodynamic psychotherapy.

    d. Advising that the Candidate's Professional Statement referred to practices that fell significantly outside his education and training, and therefore needed to be accounted for.

    e. Advising that the Candidate's "unique" approach to treatment, which fell outside of any generally recognized traditions of intervention within clinical psychology, would not be acceptable.

    f. Advising a mentee to demonstrate both a broad base in the specialty of clinical psychology as well as particular areas of interest rather than focusing too narrowly only on a specific skill.

    g. Advising that the proposed demonstration of a neuropsychological screening for possible head injury assessment using only one brief screening instrument would not be acceptable.

12. Mentors are not responsible for mentees successfully obtaining the Clinical ABPP. Whether a candidate passes the oral examination is determined completely on the basis of the candidate's own

materials and exam performance. Mentors do not certify mentees' readiness to take the examination or the applicant's likelihood of passing the examination. If requested, mentors may offer their own comments regarding an applicant's professional strengths and weaknesses.

13. The comments and advice of mentors are not communicated to ABCP or to examiners, have no bearing on the examination outcome, and may not be used to appeal an examination outcome. Mentors should never give candidates advice that the candidate could construe as representing the views of the Examining Board or advice about the Professional Statement or Practice Samples that the candidate could construe as approval or as meeting the standards of ABCP for Board Certification, since this can lead to appeals of failed exams citing that the mentor assured the mentee that the material would pass. The mentor should not be involved in the examination itself, or its outcome, with the single exception of helping the failed candidate to understand the written feedback provided by the panel and to discuss with the candidate what steps might be taken in preparing for reexamination.

14. Mentors are advised to keep e-mails or other records of interaction with mentees so that any concerns about the mentoring process can be reviewed if necessary.

15. Questions about the mentoring process, unusual circumstances, or concerns while mentoring should be referred to the Academy's Mentoring Coordinator or the President.

MENTORING COORDINATOR

1. The Mentoring Coordinator shall maintain a record of all mentees, including date of first contact, name, e-mail address, mentor assigned, employment type, city and state, whether regular or Senior Option, and the date of Board Certification.

2. The Mentoring Coordinator shall maintain a list of all mentors, how many mentees they have mentored (past and present), and outcome of mentee evaluations.

3. The Mentoring Coordinator shall collect written Evaluation Forms from all mentees after their Oral Examination, whether or not the

mentee passed. The Mentoring Coordinator shall send an Evaluation form each year from the time a mentor was assigned until the mentee has successfully obtained the ABPP or prematurely stopped the process.

4. The Mentoring Coordinator shall use the Evaluation Form not only to assess the strengths and weakness of the Academy's Mentoring Program but also to assess the strengths and weaknesses of assigned Mentors.

5. If a Mentor receives a negative evaluation from a mentee, the Mentoring Coordinator shall contact the Mentor to discuss whatever problems may have occurred in the mentoring process. If a Mentor repeatedly receives negative evaluations from different mentees, the Mentoring Coordinator may choose, along with Board approval, to not further use that individual in the Mentoring Program.

Reprinted from *The Bulletin of the American Academy of Clinical Psychology* (2012, Volume 13, Number 1) by the American Academy of Clinical Psychology by permission of the Board of Directors of the American Academy of Clinical Psychology, Inc.

Appendix B: Example Contextual Statement for an Intervention Submission

*T*he following is an example of a Contextual Statement for a video Practice Sample on intervention. It is of the same case as the hypothetical orals interaction also presented in Appendix C. (Another sample Contextual Statement is presented on www.abpp.org. Click on Specialty Boards, then on Clinical Psychology, then on "click here" at the bottom of that long page on Clinical, and look on the upper right for the samples offered there.) The example provided here is simply that—an example—and is not offered as something that necessarily exemplifies a passed exam.

These are the content requirements for the intervention Contextual Statement, from the current (2011) Manual (American Board of Clinical Psychology, 2011):

- Dates of contacts, current session number in total sequence
- Non-identifying descriptive information and history
- Presenting problem
- Course of treatment
- Diagnosis
- Theoretical and empirical rationale for interventions used
- Goals for present intervention
- Formulation and discussion of the intervention in terms of identified theory of practice
- Relevant research
- Discussion of the individual and cultural diversity and ethical/legal considerations involved
- Reflective comment on the candidate's own behavior and the interpersonal interactions in the sample

▓ A copy of the full professional written report (if applicable)
▓ Attestation that written informed consent was secured

CLIENT INFORMATION

A. is a 19-year-old African American male from a broken home who finished high school but had been involved peripherally with a neighborhood gang and was in the county's juvenile hall twice—once due to an extended absence of his mother from home and once due to an arrest for burglary. He had been referred several years before to this therapist by a juvenile hall worker but had only recently decided that he wanted to turn his life around. He was prickly and suspicious of the therapist but was motivated enough to come and find out if help might be available.

A. had two younger siblings who were still with his mother, and he tried to "help them out" with troubles as they arose. He was living with several roommates and working at a fast food restaurant. He was not currently on probation and did not currently have any involvement with the justice system.

A. was treated weekly, individually, for 1 year, with an "Acceptance and Commitment Therapy" orientation. The video was taken at the 9-month point in treatment (11-6-11; session 40 out of 59).

A.'s presenting problem was a desire to make his life better. He did not want to be trapped in a "ghetto life" with no future. He experienced mild to moderate depression (sadness, cynicism, hopelessness, and resentful anger), which appeared to be for the most part situationally related. The major obstacles to fulfilling his desire for change that emerged in treatment were (1) fear of failure and prejudice, (2) lack of confidence in his basic worth and value, and (3) anger and resentment regarding his situation.

Basically, A. was so hurt and disappointed in almost all authority figures that his primary response to life was cynical and pessimistic. He tried being part of a gang, but the gangs expressed their disappointments in violence, which he shied away from. He had enough empathy to be able to feel the pain of those who were hurt by violence or rejection, so he didn't like hurting others. His juvenile hall experiences had given him a glimpse of people who believed that life could be better, although he couldn't take much advantage of it at that time, not trusting anyone to be a stable part of his life.

DIAGNOSIS

Axis I 311.00 Depressive disorder NOS, moderate

Axis II V71.09 No diagnosis on Axis II

Axis III none

Axis IV Problems related to the social environment (life constraints of racial prejudice, few friends, unsatisfactory living condition, inadequate social support)

Axis V GAF 58 (current). (Some might have diagnosed "paranoid traits" and "antisocial traits" on Axis II, but those appeared to me to be situational behaviors or appropriate responses to his situation, rather than ingrained personality traits.)

COURSE OF TREATMENT

The first part of the treatment involved trust and getting him to recognize and share his disappointment and anger. He had a habitual suspicion of White people, which he naturally felt with me, but I did my best to be completely honest and responsible with him and willing to look nonjudgmentally at everything about him and his situation. He had angry outbursts toward me a few times, which were really about his past hurts, but I understood empathically where he was coming from, and that eventually increased his trust. One time he walked out on a session, which was painful for both of us, but once again, dealing with that helped the trust.

In establishing a therapeutic alliance, I addressed the issue of race toward the end of our first session, asking how he felt about seeing a White male. I asked if he would prefer an African American therapist, but he said that the people that he had had some meaningful connection with in juvenile hall were White, so it was okay.

I did awareness or mindfulness exercises with him in session, including internal focusing and focused meditation, and he did these daily at home, too. These exercises helped him learn a "stepping back and observing" stance. I encouraged him to accept all of his thoughts and feelings, no matter how painful or "bad." He was skeptical at first but came to appreciate the added sense of "okayness" that acceptance gave him.

To help him overcome the blockages he experienced from years of prejudice and felt unfairness, I encouraged his anger about unfairness, and helped him to accept all of his feelings about the problem (anger and shame). We worked on alternative responses and on how he came across to others, so that he could to some extent control how others reacted to him. I focused in every session on his self-respect and self-supporting behaviors, so that his self-image gradually changed to a positive one.

As he came to trust me and as he came to have hope for his future, his depression lessened, and there was no need for interventions specifically aimed at depression.

There were no ethical or legal issues of note during our work together.

In terms of outside resources, I encouraged him to take advantage of church resources, and after 6 months, he attended a youth group meeting at a church. He found a couple of guys there his own age who were unhappy over their situation as young, black males, and that contact was helpful. There were no other males in the family that could help or be good influences.

By the time we got around to dealing with values (an important aspect of ACT), he was hopeful enough to be able to espouse some positive values, like honesty, responsibility, and treating other people well. He really wanted a girlfriend whom he could trust and have the closeness with that he'd never had before. This was frightening, of course, but very motivating.

Over time, he began taking risks with outside relationships. Fortunately he was living in a decent area. We had begun to discuss career hopes and issues, and after this session we worked on preparing him emotionally for vocational or college training in the future.

A. made very significant progress during the treatment, and I'm very hopeful that he will complete some vocational training and be able to support himself proudly. From a psychodynamic point of view, he will probably have some rough times before he works through his maternal anger, but I think he can use the skills we have worked on to examine and moderate his reactions and learn to get beyond his transference feelings.

CURRENT INTERVENTION

This session focused on the client's feelings about prejudice he had encountered (and still encounters, of course) and the despair that this had engendered in him. The goal of this work was to eventually free him from self-doubt and distracting anger engendered by constant prejudice and to give him an adaptive way to deal with such things in the future.

I encouraged his anger about unfairness and prejudice and accepted his feelings, legitimizing them as appropriate, and trying to convey my respect for him. We worked on his self-rejection because of the attitudes of prejudice against him. As his anger faded, I helped him practice softer responses to prejudice and suspicion, including some humor and even humorous self-deprecation. We talked about what his manner, demeanor, movements, and clothing communicated to others (e.g., wearing hoodies in public).

THEORETICAL AND EMPIRICAL RATIONALE FOR INTERVENTIONS USED

Acceptance and Commitment Therapy (ACT) is a cognitive-behavioral therapy that holds that we identify too much with and "reify" our experience (our thoughts and feelings), and that we put too much emphasis on evaluating our experience as "good" or "bad." We make great efforts to give "reasons" for our thoughts and feelings, which are usually rationalizations rather than the truth. The theory is that directly resisting internal problems (generally by using the traditional defenses) keeps the real problem underground. Clients are helped to relax that defensive struggle and to actually feel what's going on, so that that information can then be used to enhance motivation to change and to act in ways that will lessen the problem.

ACT advocates stepping back to view our thoughts, feelings, and other experiences as part of a never-ending flow of experience that is always changing, rather than something that must always be taken seriously and that routinely requires immediate response. Some research is showing that this mindful detachment itself can have some good effects on people, like less anxiety, more balance, and so forth. ACT also focuses on making sure that actions are consistent with our values, rather than impulsive.

Formulation and Discussion of the Intervention in Terms of Identified Theory of Practice and Relevant Research

ACT research began with its founding in 2003, and there are some important findings already. ACT is classified as an empirically supported treatment for pain, and I think it will soon be for other symptoms as well. A lot of the work has been conducted in Nevada by Hayes and his group, and there are others exploring it, too. Zettle, Rains, and Hayes (2011) looked at whether the effective mechanisms of ACT are the same as those of CBT in general, and found as a side point that ACT was more effective than standard CBT for some purposes. Some techniques in Positive Psychology lately fit well with ACT, such as gratitude and forgiveness.

SELF-REFLECTION

Transferentially, I think A. needed both a nurturing father figure and a corrective maternal experience. I tried to provide some of both for him, by being honest, responsible, accepting, and encouraging.

His anger and initial suspiciousness did not bother me, since I was secure in knowing that I was being as transparent and honest with him as possible, and I understood empathically that his suspiciousness was entirely justified by his life experience. I did not feel any pull or desire on my part to coddle him or protect him from reality, which is related to my strong belief that facing the truth is essential for therapy.

REFERENCES

American Board of Clinical Psychology. (2011). *Examination manual for board certification in clinical psychology for the American board of professional psychology.* Retrieved from www.abpp.org/files/page-specific/3355%20Clinical/15_ABCP_Exam_Manual .pdf

Zettle, R. D., Rains, J. C., & Hayes, S. C. (2011). Do acceptance and commitment therapy and cognitive therapy for depression work via the same process: A reanalysis of Zettle and Rains, 1989. *Behavior Modification, 35,* 265–283.

Appendix C: Exam Excerpt on Intervention Practice Sample

A hypothetical excerpt from an exam is presented below, from that part of the exam concerning an intervention Practice Sample. This is the same case that was presented in Appendix B, to familiarize you with what may be the style of most orals (every one of which is different, of course, even within the same general schedule of the exam). The questions asked by the examiners here are reasonably typical. The answers given by the candidate are unique and are not intended to portray "good" or "passing" answers. You can make your own judgments from the principles presented in the orals chapter.

The case was of a 19-year-old African American male from a broken home who had finished high school but had been involved peripherally with a neighborhood gang and had been in the county's juvenile hall twice—once due to an extended absence of his mother from home and once due to an arrest for burglary. He had been referred several years before to this therapist by a juvenile hall worker but had only recently decided that he wanted to turn his life around. He was prickly and suspicious of the therapist but was motivated enough to come and find out if help might be available. He was treated weekly for 1 year, with an "Acceptance and Commitment Therapy" orientation. The video was taken at the 9-month point in treatment and the session focused on the client's feelings about prejudice he encountered and the despair for his future that that prejudice had engendered in him for years. In what follows, the examiners are labeled E1, E2, and E3, and the examinee is C.

E1: You say that you treated this client with an "Acceptance and Commitment Therapy" method, but I don't think any of us on the panel are very familiar with that. Can you explain the basics for us?

C: Acceptance and Commitment Therapy (ACT) has been in the literature and practiced for about 10 years now. My first exposure was Steven Hayes' book on the subject, which I found to be very stimulating, because the approach makes use of some psychological insights that are more "philosophical" and less symptom focused than the CBT commonly taught now. The symptom-focused treatments made sense to me and seemed to work with many clients, but I believe that psychotherapy should be about a person's life as a whole, whenever possible, and not just about getting rid of symptoms. I know that that may not be a popular view with insurance companies, but I dislike the fact that helping clients is so limited by insurance payments, which is quite a separate topic, I realize.

ACT's basic ideas are that we identify too much with and "reify" our experience—our thoughts and feelings, and that we put too much emphasis on evaluating our experience as good or bad. We try to avoid the bad instead of managing or dealing with it, and we make great efforts to give "reasons" for our thoughts and feelings, which are usually rationalizations rather than the truth. So, ACT advocates taking our thoughts, feelings, and other experiences less seriously, and developing the capacity to step back and view them as they occur, as something that is just happening in us rather than something that requires immediate response. This is similar to what people do in meditation (at least mindfulness meditation, which is the only one I'm familiar with), and some research is showing that that mindful detachment itself can have some good effects on people, like less anxiety, more balance, and so forth.

I try to help clients (when this approach is appropriate, of course) to be aware of their inner experience, to observe it, and to take a slower and more considered approach to taking action. I also focus with the client on making sure that his actions are consistent with his or her values, rather than more impulsive, and of course this means that the client must know clearly what his values are to start with, so we explore that area, too.

E2: It sounds like the goals of psychodynamic therapies, so what's different here?

C: Looking at the client's life and functioning as a whole may be similar, but in ACT we employ specific activities and homework that teach the client functional skills that help deal with any issue. The most important of these skills are the stepping back to see and understand one's own behavior and acceptance rather than fighting oneself about one's experience.

E2: Do you do anything about traditional symptoms or just let them fade out?

C: ACT is technically a cognitive-behavioral therapy, so for instance, if special attention to anxiety or depression is needed, I do use some more traditional CBT techniques within the larger ACT treatment.

E3: Doesn't "acceptance" imply just living with your symptoms or whatever psychological pain is occurring?

C: Not really. The theory is that directly resisting internal problems is generally done by using the traditional defenses, most especially denial, suppression, and repression, which keeps the real problem underground. The acceptance I promote with clients helps them to relax that defensive struggle, to actually feel what's going on, and to use information to promote motivation, change, or act in ways that will lessen the problem. So I'm not asking them to "get used to it" and live with it ultimately but rather to stop their usual avoidances, rationalizations, and struggles against it and to learn new ways of coping. And, we know that recognizing and observing one's pain does lessen it a little anyway, even without the better coping techniques.

E1: Is there research support for ACT?

C: Yes, just since 2003, but there are some important findings already. ACT is classified as an empirically supported treatment for pain, and I think it soon will be for other symptoms as well. A lot of the work has been done in Nevada by Hayes and his group, but there are others at work, too.

E1: What is some recent research that you are familiar with?

C: I've been looking at applicable techniques in Positive Psychology lately, mostly developed by Seligman and his group in Pennsylvania. I think the gratitude and forgiveness concepts are quite useful in ACT, and I bring these to the attention of most clients, when it is the right time. Zettle, Rains, and Hayes (2011) recently looked at whether the effective mechanisms of ACT are the same as those of CBT in general, and found as a side point that ACT was more effective than standard CBT for some purposes. I also go to the meetings of the Association for Behavioral and Cognitive Therapy, which always have presentations on ACT.

E2: How does ACT apply to or adjust to persons of diversity?

C: Well, the part about getting used to dealing with people with backgrounds different from your own and learning to relate to people from various backgrounds in ways that are culturally educated and sensitive are the same, no matter what your orientation is, so that's no different. I think people of all diverse backgrounds, or really all backgrounds, are pretty unaware of how they process inner experience, and I find that people, uniformly, know nothing about trying acceptance, so it doesn't seem like people of certain ethnic backgrounds, for example, are any more resistant to it than everyone else. Maybe Latinos are a little more resistant to the use of acceptance, and Asians are a little more familiar with meditation, but it doesn't seem to matter very much. You do see some differences in values when we do that part of the treatment— I mean identifying values clearly so that actions taken can be consistent with and in part motivated by those values. People's values are somewhat different in different cultures, but I'm not concerned with changing them, just identifying them so we can work with them.

E1: I'm hearing the acceptance part, but what about it is the "commitment" part of the name?

C: ACT puts considerable emphasis on knowing what you want and taking action to go in that direction, so the commitment part is identifying your motivation and connecting your values and needs with your actions. It's a little like motivational interviewing, in that if the client isn't naturally hooking up his values and needs with his actions, we explore what's missing. Sometimes people hold back out of fear of failure or not feeling that they deserve success, and we have to work on those issues.

E1: Your contextual statement explained this, but can you summarize for us again your conceptualization of the client's treatment in your practice sample?

C: Sure. Basically, he was so hurt and disappointed in almost all authority figures that his primary response to life was cynical and pessimistic. Given his environment growing up and his mother's unpredictable absences, it was natural that he would be largely negative about everything and would try out the gang scene. Fortunately, the gangs were even more negative than he was, and they expressed their disappointments in violence, which he shied away from. He had enough empathy to be able to feel the pain of those who were hurt by violence or rejection, so he didn't like hurting others. This just left him stuck in his hopeless cynicism, though. His juvenile hall experiences had given him a glimpse of people who believed that life could be better, although he couldn't take much advantage of it at that time, not trusting anyone to "be there" and not be out of his life soon.

The first part of the treatment involved trust, of course, and getting him to recognize and share his disappointment and anger. Me being White didn't help, but I just did my best to be completely honest and responsible with him, and willing to look non-judgmentally at everything about him. He had angry outbursts at me a few times, which were really about his hurt, but I certainly understood empathically where he was coming from, and that helped the trust. When he wouldn't talk about his feelings or past experiences, I focused on his motivation— what he wanted out of the treatment, and that usually got him going again. One time he walked out, which was painful for both of us, but once again, it helped the trust ultimately.

We did awareness or mindfulness exercises, pretty much like simple meditation, in session, and I had him do them daily, too, which he actually did. I think it offered him a chance at control, which he had so little of in his life overall. This led naturally to the stepping back and observing stance and we used those observations in session a lot. I frequently brought up the notion of accepting his thoughts and feelings, no matter how painful or "bad," and we worked on that.

He was skeptical at first, of course, but the relaxing that comes with not defending or fighting the truth anymore is a positive experience for almost everyone, so he caught on after a while.

By the time we got to values, he was softened up enough emotionally to be able to espouse some positive values, like honesty, responsibility, and treating other people well. He really wanted a girlfriend, too, or actually, he wanted girlfriend that he could trust and have the closeness with that he'd never had before. That was scary, of course, but very motivating.

Over time, he began taking risks with outside relationships. Fortunately he was living in a decent area. We have begun to discuss career hopes and issues, and I hope that he will begin some vocational or college training in the future.

E2: How did you handle the race issue?

C: In our relationship or in his experience in the world?

E2: Both, actually.

C: In establishing a therapeutic alliance, I addressed the issue toward the end of our first session, asking how he felt about seeing a White male. I was quite comfortable with him, because I sensed immediately that he was serious about changing his life and that he was not needing to hurt other people in order to deal with his feelings. I asked if he would prefer an African American therapist, but he said that the people that he had had some meaningful connection with in juvenile hall were White, so it was okay.

With regard to his dealing with the race issue, I encouraged his anger about unfairness and accepted his feelings, legitimizing them as appropriate, and trying to convey my respect for him and what he was wanting to do so that he could start accepting his various feelings—anger but also shame. You know—self-rejection because of the attitudes of prejudice against him. As the anger diminished we could focus on doing something about the prejudice, and I helped him practice softer responses including some humor and even humorous self-deprecation expressed to people who shied away from him. We talked about impression management, what his manner, demeanor, movements, and clothing communicated, so that he could choose the messages he wanted to send. As he gained some self-respect through our relationship, he stopped wearing hoodies, for obvious reasons.

E1: At one point on the tape, the client expresses considerable anger about the way people in general react to him as a young African American male, and you just sat there in silence for a while. He then asked for a response, and you spoke, but I'm wondering why you sat there in silence after what was clearly a highly emotional moment.

C: I believe in truth in psychotherapy, and that is consistent with ACT's behavioral emphasis on what is. I suppose many therapists would have responded right away with soothing or supportive or encouraging responses, but I think that those are usually efforts to get away from the client's emotion and diminish the client's pain, and they are usually rationalizations of some kind, almost like saying "There, there, it will be all right." Actually, this young man is going to live with those negative stereotypes and reactions on the part of many people around him for the rest of his life. I think that is serious enough to need a serious response, which at that point was basically "Yes, that's how it is, and that's how it's going to be with some people." We had been through that issue a number of times already in other sessions, and I had encouraged his anger and his recognition of the realities of the situation. So, this time, I didn't need to do that, and I sat there, trying to just be accepting, since ultimately I want him to be more accepting about the issue. When I finally spoke, I think I said something like "Yes, your anger about unfairness is totally justified, and it's something you are going to have to make your peace with some time."

E3: Don't you view that anger as a problem, if he goes around outside of therapy being angry toward others?

C: Not really, since he doesn't turn it into violence or displace it into non-prejudice situations. If he gets rejection on the basis of his skin color and age, then I think he has some right to try to at least tell people they don't have to be afraid of him. Of course, I hope he'll learn fairly soon, and I will help him learn, more subtle responses that may change some people's minds about him.

E3: What do you think happens in his system of understanding things when you or he "accept" something? For instance, if he does become less angry at the prejudice that affects his life, do you think he has to reconceptualize something or reframe something, so that he has a different cognitive frame of reference for responding to those behaviors in the future?

C: Well, sure, there will be some reframing.

E3: Do you help shape those reframes, or do you think they "just happen" and it doesn't matter what their form is?

C: I do offer possible ways of reframing things, but it's up to him to choose how he wants to do it. I prefer more compassion-oriented reframes, making "allowances" for people's hurtful behaviors. So, I might suggest understanding those prejudice-based behaviors as coming from fear and ignorance (but without ignoring the obvious associations, like fear when a White person sees a group of young Black men in a ghetto area giving them a "hard" look), and I would suggest a compassionate view of that fear and ignorance, since a compassionate response will lead eventually to less fear and ignorance.

E3: If he tried to dampen his anger by viewing prejudiced people as automatons, essentially non-human and therefore ignorant, would you object?

C: I would point out that this view will make it easier for him to harm them back, so that if he wants to harm them back, that might work, but I would point out that harming them back will lead to more fear and prejudice, even if it feels good.

E2: Did you employ any non-ACT techniques, like for depression?

C: No, it wasn't necessary. He readily accepted and gained from my respect for him and really wasn't depressed deep down, not nearly as much as I thought he would be.

E1: Did you look for any family or community resources that could help him?

C: That's a good point. I encouraged him to take advantage of church resources, and after 6 months, he attended a youth group meeting at a church. He found a couple of guys there his own age who were unhappy over their situation as young, Black males, and that contact was helpful. I checked on other males in the family that could help or be good influences, but there just weren't any.

E1: It sounds like you rely a good deal on the relationship with clients to get across your message about acceptance and commitment.

C: Yes, that's true. Clients have to believe that you see the truth of their lives and their struggles and that you still believe that things can be better. I think that comes across in choice of words, inflections, and body language, and how you treat them as human beings.

E1: How would your treatment of this client be different if you were using relationship therapy?

C: Well, I'm not particularly versed in relationship therapy, but I think it would focus more exclusively on the elements of relationship between the therapist and client, more of a transference/countertransference treatment plus exploring all of the emotional reactions each party is having to the other, and why. This would have been pretty much the same for the rapport-building and trust-building parts of my treatment, but I don't know if relationship therapy would include as much specific teaching, focus on learning acceptance, and taking considered action outside the therapy.

E2: Now that countertransference has been brought up, what were you aware of in that respect with this client?

C: I think his transference reactions were largely paternal with me, since he had never had a father and since his mother was a very ambivalent figure to him, due to her abandonments. I think that I provided a reasonably good father figure for him, being honest, responsible, accepting, and encouraging. Probably some of his expressed anger related, at least tangentially, to anger at fathers for not being there for him at all.

As I said, I respected very much his determination to better his life and his willingness to risk in coming to therapy. His anger and initial suspiciousness did not bother me, since I was secure in knowing that I was being as transparent and honest with him as possible, and I understood empathically that his suspiciousness was entirely justified by his life experience.

I'm sure that I unconsciously encouraged his trait of not wanting to take out his disappointments on others. I really wanted him to succeed, since so few boys from his background even try to rise above their circumstances and many end up in lives of crime. I don't think that my wish for him to succeed distorted the therapy very much, if at all, but I could just be unaware of such effects, I suppose. I know that I did not feel any pull or desire on my part to coddle him or protect him from reality, and I'm sure this is related to my strong belief that facing the truth is essential for therapy.

From a psychodynamic point of view, he will probably have some rough times before he works through his maternal anger, but I think he can use the skills we have worked on to examine and moderate his reactions and learn to get beyond his transference feelings.

REFERENCE

Zettle, R. D., Rains, J. C., & Hayes, S. C. (2011). Do acceptance and commitment therapy and cognitive therapy for depression work via the same process: A reanalysis of Zettle and Rains (1989). *Behavior Modification, 35,* 265–283.

Appendix D: Exam Excerpt From Ethics and Legal Foundations

A hypothetical excerpt from an exam is presented below, from that part of the exam concerning ethics and legal foundations, to familiarize you with what may be the style of most orals (every one of which is different, of course, even within the same general schedule of the exam). The questions asked by the examiners here are reasonably typical. The answers given by the candidate are unique and are not intended to portray "good" or "passing" answers. You can make your own judgments from the principles presented in the orals chapter.

E1: Your ethical dilemma described in your Professional Statement was about whether to report a colleague who you knew was "fudging" diagnoses in order to ensure insurance payment. Can you recap that for us?

C: Yes. I learned about it by noticing in our shared office his billing diagnosis for a particular client and knowing that it was not the same as the case when he described it in our peer consultation group. I asked him about it, and he said that the insurance for that client wouldn't pay for the real diagnosis, so he used a diagnosis that would be paid. This could be considered a symptomatic diagnosis for the client but was not the primary diagnosis and not what my colleague was focusing on in the sessions. If the insurance company had seen his notes, I suppose they would have noticed the discrepancy.

I didn't say any more at the time, although it bothered me somewhat. Then I noticed the same thing again with another of his clients. He didn't seem concerned about hiding it, and I presumed he didn't think it was a big deal. I was pretty sure it was unethical, and I checked the ethics code (American Psychological Association (2010)) and thought about it some more. I didn't feel right about that going on in our office, although it was not a corporation, just a group of people sharing the rent, but I was also concerned that he might end up getting in trouble over that kind of thing, so I decided to take the first step described in the ethics code for such situations and talk to him about it as an ethics issue. That didn't go very well. He resented my pointing it out, of course, and his argument was that when he did do this, he did his best to use diagnoses that were in a sense true for the client, even though they were not his focus of treatment. My argument was that sessions are authorized on the basis of what is actually being treated, so he was getting authorizations (and payments) by lying, and I was worried that he would have trouble over it. He did not seem inclined to change doing that, as it could seriously affect his income.

I continued to worry about this not being resolved, and I considered notifying the American Psychological Association (APA) ethics committee or the state licensing board. Our state psychological association ethics committee has given up any real authority and just tries to "educate." I figured that if I used APA, he might end up losing his membership, but if I notified the licensing board, he could lose his license, which would be worse. I didn't know whether APA notifies the licensing boards when they find that someone has violated the ethics code or if they only do that in certain kinds of cases, like sexual violations. I had just decided to notify APA ethics when we saw in our licensing board's newsletter notice of someone else losing his or her license for using secondary diagnoses for billing, and fortunately, he was scared enough that he vowed to stop doing it. After that I didn't see any more evidence of it, though of course it might have been hidden. I figured that I didn't need to do any more, and I was glad that he stopped doing it.

E1: Did you try to check with APA about whether they do notify licensing boards?

C: No, I could have, but I thought that it was serious enough that I was going to tell them anyway. At that point, I started worrying also that if I didn't report it anywhere, if it became known by our licensing board that I had not reported it, they might see it as collusion or an ethical failure on my part. They seem unpredictable that way.

E2: You mentioned the state psychological association's ethics committee. Did you consider reporting it to them, for an "educational" effort on their part, which might have seemed serious enough to your colleague that he would have stopped doing it then?

C: Well, that would have been a possibility, but I thought that to him that would seem just like other colleagues talking to him, just like I had, and he was so unresponsive to that that I thought it wouldn't have worked.

E2: You could have tried it, though, to see if it would work.

C: Yes, you're right. Looking back now, my annoyance at his putting me off when I talked to him about it may have entered into my decision to go to the APA rather than to the state psychological association. It does seem more strategic if I had done the state psychological thing first.

E1: Were you prepared to deal with fall-out from him if it had been reported and he knew that you had done so?

C: I thought that he would be angry, and I dreaded that, but I felt strongly enough about things like that that are unethical that I thought I might ride it out in the office by arguing that it was better for him to be convinced to stop doing it, even if it took an outside organization to do it. If that had not been feasible, I figured I could change offices, and I was willing to do that if that was necessary. It would have been a problem for our peer consultation group, of course, but I couldn't prevent that.

E2: Did you consider bringing it up in the peer consultation group, to see if that might convince him to stop?

C: That would have been the simplest course to take, but I thought that that might cause trouble in the whole office, and I thought that as long as APA accepted his apologies and his promise to stop doing it, it might not be made public, and that that kind of trouble in the office could be avoided.

E1: Looking back now, might you have chosen another course?

C: I'm thinking as we talk about it, that it was mostly an avoidance of conflict on my part that I didn't bring it up in the peer consultation group first, I mean after I had talked to him about it. I tend to avoid conflict in general, and I was a little surprised at myself that I might actually report this thing rather than avoid it altogether. I could have hoped that some peer pressure from the group would have worked. Then, if it hadn't, I could use the state psychological association ethics group to see if that would work before going further. He probably wouldn't have been any madder if I had done that versus going to APA first.

ETHICAL VIGNETTE FROM COMMITTEE

You are working with a mother, father, and child regarding the child's bedwetting. During the course of your treatment, the 10-year-old child tells you that a friend of his has had bruises that he said were the result of his parents' correcting his bad behavior with a large wooden paddle. You ask some questions, and he says he has seen similar bruises before on this child. He tells you the name of the child and roughly where he lives. Do you take any action?

[10 minutes for candidate to think about the vignette]

C: The child abuse law in my state does not distinguish abuse of a child client from abuse of a non-client, when that information is learned in the course of one's practice, and I have heard that bruises are evidence of abuse, even if they are from spanking. So, I would call Child Protective Services anonymously first, and confirm these understandings. Assuming they were confirmed, I would let my client and his parents know that I was going to make a mandated report. Then I would make the report, by phone, followed by a form.

E1: How would you deal with the child's sense of violated confidentiality due to your report?

C: I always explain to children at the first or second session that I will try to keep what he or she says confidential but that there may be times when I have to share something with someone else, and I will use my judgment in regard to whether it is necessary to share it. I specifically mention their parents as well as the school and the government agency that protects children from abuse. I tell them that I will share information that I learn that indicates that the child's welfare or safety is at risk, like if the child were to say that he was planning to imitate a beloved superhero and jump off of the roof of the house to fly, or if he told me that someone was bullying him at school and stealing his lunch money. I tell them that I would also share information that indicated that a sibling or friend was at risk or in danger. So, I would explain my report in this context and discuss his feelings about it, especially about how it might affect his friendship with this other boy.

E1: Do you think you are obligated to let the parents know about the friend's abuse?

C: I tell the parents the same thing that I tell the child about preserving the child's confidentiality. I don't think I would be obligated to let the parents know about the abuse per se, but I would want them to know that I was reporting regarding the specific friend of their child, in case that child's parents became aware of where the information came from. I believe that Child Protective Services does not give out the name of a reporter unless they have to, or something like that. I'm not sure why they would have to, maybe in court or something?

E3: What if it were the case that a report on a non-client child was not mandated in your state? Would you be motivated to report, or would you take any other action?

C: If I wasn't sure whether a report on a non-client child was mandated, I would consult an attorney. Then when I was sure that it was not mandated, I would probably tell the parents about the information and suggest that they report it if they want to. If they did not wish to, I would suggest that they tell the school about it. If they still did not want to act, I would ask them for permission to report it to the school myself, since the school is a mandated reporter. If they refused permission, I would probably let it drop, since I personally do not like the concept of non-mandated reporting. I believe optional reporting opens up too much option for people to report more than is really appropriate. There have to be some limits on what we expect of parents in terms of perfect parenting.

E3: What do you think should be mandated?

C: I think things are okay the way they are, with serious abuse or risks being required reports.

E2: Do you have an opinion about "emotional abuse"? Should it be a mandated report?

C: I dislike any intentional hurting of another person, and emotional abuse certainly qualifies. Destroying a child's self-esteem by intentional negative statements about the child is cruel and harmful, but

I'm ambivalent about specific restrictions on public speech, like those offensive-speech laws being adopted some places in Europe. I guess I do think that higher levels of emotional abuse should be reported.

E2: What level of emotional abuse should be reported?

C: Well, repeated, chronic belittling and put-downs should be reportable, but occasional ones should not be. That would be a difficult threshold to use, of course. I also think that the penalties for those parents should not include incarceration. Probably the best thing would be required therapy for the child until he or she is 18 years old.

E1: I notice that you say you don't like optional reporting, but you also said that you would inform the school with the parents' permission. Is that inconsistent?

C: I guess it reflects my ambivalence about optional reporting. I think the bruises are significant evidence of a situation that needs some attention, and if no one disagrees (like the child or the parents) about doing so, I would do it. But if anyone did not want me to inform the school, because of consequences they foresaw for themselves, then I would let it go.

E1: Do you have any particular method you use to figure out what to do when there are ethical-legal questions?

C: Well, I do, actually. I think first about each party involved, including myself, and what duties—ethical, legal, and moral—that I have to each. Then I study the ethics code and relevant laws for information. After that I write down each possible scenario for my action and write down who benefits or doesn't from each. The most important priority is my client's welfare. Studying that usually brings me to the best decision I can make, and finally I make sure that what seems to be the best decision actually "feels" right. If I'm still unsure, I consult with a colleague or, if necessary, an attorney.

REFERENCE

American Psychological Association. (2010). *Ethical principles of psychologists and code of conduct.* Washington, DC: American Psychological Association. Retrieved from www .apa.org/ethics/code/index.aspx.

Index

mentors, 130
  obtaining, 31
  procedures, 131–133
  reviewing CV, 43
  types of, 41
mentorship, goals, 129–130
Millon Behavioral Health Inventory
    (MBHI), 60
Minnesota Multiphasic Personality
    Inventory-2 (MMPI-2), 60
motivation, to become Board
    Certified, 19

National Register of Health Service
    Providers in Psychology
    (NRHSPP), 37
neuropsychological impairment, 62

ongoing learning, 23
online, application process,
    35, 36
openness to collaboration
    in practice, 98
openness to differences, attitude,
    95–96
openness to improvement,
    attitude, 98
oral examination, 22, 26, 39, 93–94
  after, 116–117
  Clinical Psychologists, 95
  expected exam schedule, 94
  helpful attitudes for, 95–98
  Practice Samples, 94
  practicing, 114–116
  preparation for. *See* preparation for
    examination
  working with group to
    preparation, 31–32
organizations, programs, or agencies
    (OPA), administration of, 29

Patient Protection and Affordable
    Care Act, 112
personal development, 23
post-doctoral experience, 32, 36, 37
Practice Samples, 9, 122–123
  choosing, 34
  examination process, 20–21, 26
  recorded, 21, 22, 102
    assessment, 85–87
    complexity, 78–79
    consultation, 88
    failure, 91–92
    general considerations, 77–78
    intervention, 87–88
    mechanics, 81–83
    privacy, 80–81
    recommendations/concerns for
      specific, 84–89
    representativeness, 81
    review, 83
    scoring, 90–91
    Senior Option, 89–90
    supervision, 89
    technological concerns, 80
  setting timelines, 30
  well-written, 40
preparation for examination
  assessment sample, 102
  consultation Practice Sample,
    103–104
  CV and Professional Statement,
    99–100
  emotions, 113
  ethical and legal issues, 108–111
  examiners, 99
  general treatment process, 101
  individual and cultural diversity,
    111
  intervention sample, 103
  professional identification, 112–113
  recorded Practice Samples and
    Contextual Statements, 102